HEROES OF HISTORY

THOMAS EDISON

Inspiration and Hard Work

HEROES OF HISTORY

THOMAS EDISON

Inspiration and Hard Work

JANET & GEOFF BENGE

Emerald
Books

P.O. BOX 635, LYNNWOOD, WA 98046

Emerald Books are distributed through YWAM Publishing. For a full list of titles, including other great biographies, visit our website at www.emeraldbooks.com.

Library of Congress Cataloging-in-Publication Data

Benge, Janet, 1958–
   Thomas Edison : inspiration and hard work / by Janet and Geoff Benge.
      p. cm. — (Heroes of history)
   Includes bibliographical references.
   ISBN-13: 978-1-932096-37-8 (pbk.)
   ISBN-10: 1-932096-37-X (pbk.)
   1. Edison, Thomas A. (Thomas Alva), 1847–1931—Juvenile literature. 2. Inventors—United States—Biography—Juvenile literature. 3. Electric engineers—United States—Biography—Juvenile literature. I. Benge, Geoff, 1954– II. Title.
   TK140.E3B46 2007
   621.3092—dc22
   [B]   2007005939

Thomas Edison: Inspiration and Hard Work
Copyright © 2007 by Janet and Geoff Benge

Published by Emerald Books
P.O. Box 635
Lynnwood, WA 98046

ISBN 978-1-932096-37-8 (paperback)
ISBN 978-1-932096-89-7 (e-book)

Second printing 2015

Printed in the United States of America

HEROES OF HISTORY

Biographies

Abraham Lincoln
Alan Shepard
Ben Carson
Benjamin Franklin
Billy Graham
Christopher Columbus
Clara Barton
Davy Crockett
Daniel Boone
Douglas MacArthur
Elizabeth Fry
George Washington
George Washington Carver
Harriet Tubman
John Adams
John Smith
Laura Ingalls Wilder
Louis Zamperini
Meriwether Lewis
Milton Hershey
Orville Wright
Ronald Reagan
Theodore Roosevelt
Thomas Edison
William Penn
William Wilberforce

Available in paperback, e-book, and audiobook formats.
Unit Study Curriculum Guides are available for each biography.
www.emeraldbooks.com

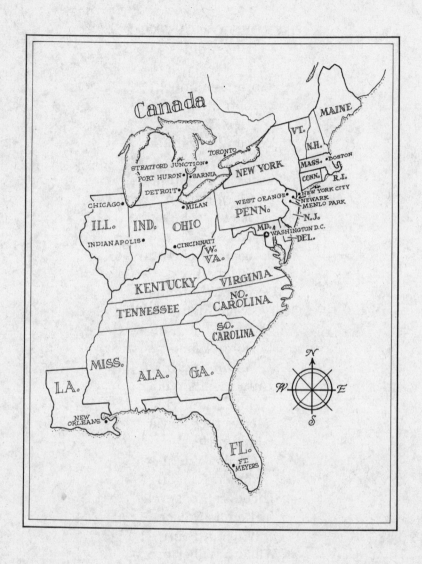

Contents

Chapter 1

A Disembodied Voice

Mary had a little lamb, its fleece was white as snow. Everywhere that Mary went, the lamb was sure to go. It followed her to school one day, which was against the rules..." The words of the children's nursery rhyme crackled forth in Thomas Edison's voice as he cranked the machine on his desk.

At the end of the nursery rhyme, the men who had gathered around Tom's desk for the demonstration were astonished and stood in stunned silence. Tom had to admit he was astonished too, not because the device had worked—Thomas knew it would eventually—but because it had worked on the first try.

The silence continued as the men grappled with what they had just heard. These men had worked with Tom on improving the telephone and were used to hearing a voice being carried over a wire. But this was different. Then, there had always been a person at the other end of the wire speaking. Now, the voice the men had just heard was disembodied. Tom was not at the end of a wire speaking into a telephone. Instead his voice had been conjured forth from the indentations on a sheet of tinfoil wrapped around a metal cylinder.

"Mein Gott in himmel!" John Krusei, the Swiss machinist who had built the device according to Tom's design, finally exclaimed in German.

A cheer then went up from the other men gathered at the table as one of the men gasped, "It's like magic!"

Tom chuckled to himself. He knew better. It wasn't like magic at all, at least not to him. The concept and design were quite simple, really. They were based upon the principles of sound waves that Tom had gleaned while working to improve the telephone. Yet despite the simplicity of the machine's concept and design, no one had ever before made such a device. That was because Tom's getting to the simple had been a long and complex process. Tom had thought about and experimented with ideas, dismissing some and altering others. Then he had experimented again until he had arrived at the design for the machine sitting on his desk, which he had dubbed the "phonograph."

But then that was how Tom worked—always thinking, always asking questions, until he arrived at the question that led him to a deep understanding or insight that he could use to develop some new invention. As far back as he could remember, Tom had always been asking questions, even as a small boy back in Milan, Ohio.

Chapter 2

Questions

Four-year-old Thomas Alva Edison, or Al, as everyone called him, skipped along the dusty street of Milan, Ohio. He was taking lunch to his father, who owned the shingle mill. It was a hot summer's day, and Al stopped to watch as several huge wagons rumbled by. His mother had told him that the wagons were called prairie schooners, and they were heading out to cross the Great Plains on their way to California to catch the tail end of the gold rush that had begun there three years before in 1848. Along the way the wagons would most likely have to fend off attacks from hostile Indians. Two young boys sat high up on the seat of the second wagon. Al wished that he could climb right up there beside them and join their great adventure westward.

The sight of the prairie schooners filled Al with more questions than he could find the answers to. What did the Great Plains look like? Did Indians really paint their faces when they went on the warpath and attacked settlers? What did gold look like in the ground? And how did they melt it down and get it to stick together in large blocks like the ones he had once seen at the bank?

Al sighed as he continued on his way along the street toward the shingle mill. Questions. Questions. Questions. He had so many questions. In fact, one of his father's workers at the mill had joked one day that it would cost Mr. Edison less to hire a man to answer all Al's questions than to have Al constantly interrupting their work to ask them about things.

The town of Milan was located on the Huron River, and a canal had been built to connect the town to Lake Erie. As a result Milan had a busy port, where grain and other commodities were loaded onto boats and barges for shipment overseas and to other American cities. In fact, Al's father, Samuel Edison, had told Al that Milan was the second largest wheat-shipping port in the world after the city of Odessa in the Ukraine, though Al was not quite sure where that was. This was another question he was in search of an answer for.

Large warehouses and grain silos lined the docks of the port, and as Al walked along, his curiosity got the better of him. He strolled over to watch a barge being loaded with grain. He was fascinated with how the grain was flowing from one of the silos into the barge. Before he knew it, he had set down the basket containing his father's lunch and was climbing up the side of the silo for a better look.

Al clambered on top of the silo and crawled over to the edge of the opening in the top. He peered inside, but it was too dark to see much. As he leaned farther inside the opening for a better look, he overbalanced and found himself tumbling headfirst into the darkness. He fell about ten feet and landed with a thud on his back on top of the mound of wheat that filled the silo. He thrashed about, trying to make it to the side of the silo where he hoped he might be able to find some handholds and pull himself back up to the opening. Instead of moving toward the side with each thrash of his arms and legs, Al found himself sinking deeper into the grain—into a sea of wheat. And of course the fear that came with this realization caused him to thrash about even harder.

"Hold on, boy! Stop moving like that, or you'll drown in wheat," a voice boomed through the darkness.

Al stopped, looked up, and saw a face peering over the edge of the opening above him.

"I'm going to lower a rope down to you. I want you to wrap it under your arms and tie a knot in it. Then I'll pull you out. Do you understand?"

"Yes," Al replied weakly. He did as he was instructed, and a few minutes later he was sitting back on top of the grain silo.

"Lucky I saw you climbing up there," the man said with a stern look on his face. "If the wheat didn't drown you, you would have suffocated from all the dust. A silo is no place for a young boy like you to be playing."

Al nodded sheepishly and then scrambled down the side of the silo, picked up his father's lunch basket, and went on his way, determined to never again see the inside of a grain silo that close. He hated to think of what his father would say when he found out about the incident. Thankfully Al was spared a whipping; his father told him that being that scared was lesson enough.

As time went on, Al had one particular question that bothered him and for which he had not yet been able to get a satisfactory answer. The question had to do with fire. Al had seen the benefits of fire all around him. His mother cooked their meals over the open hearth in the kitchen, and the house was lit at night with lanterns and candles. Al had often wished that he could take one of the lanterns down and experiment with it, but his father strictly forbade him to do so. Still, his question remained: What kind of things would fire burn? But of course one question was never enough for Al. He also wanted to know why some bits of charred wood were left when a fire died down and why some things burned faster than others.

The questions would not go away, and so late one afternoon when Al was six years old, he decided it was time to try to find the answers for himself. He crept out to the barn at the back of the Edison property. He gathered some dry sticks, which he carefully arranged into a pile in the barn. He smiled to himself with satisfaction as he struck a match and held it to the sticks, several of which began to burn. Al extinguished the match, sat back, and watched as orange tongues of flame slowly licked their way around the sticks. Soon the whole pile of wood was ablaze.

Al studied the burning pile intently to see how the flames consumed the sticks. But when he looked up, he noticed that the sticks were not the only thing burning. The straw strewn across the barn floor had also caught afire. Al jumped to his feet, and as fast and as furiously as he could, he tried to stamp out the burning straw. But it was no use. The flames were spreading too fast, and the barn was starting to fill with choking smoke. Moments later the bales of straw in the loft ignited. Al fled the burning barn.

Several passersby had noticed the smoke billowing from the barn, and a group of men carrying buckets were running down the street toward the Edison property. Moments later the men had formed a bucket line from the canal to the burning barn. Al watched as they furiously passed bucketfuls of water to one another until the buckets reached the burning barn. But he could see that the men's efforts were futile. Al had managed to set the whole barn ablaze, and the roof was caving in. He hoped that the fire did not spread any further. He was sure that he was already in a lot of trouble, but he couldn't imagine how much more trouble he would be in if the flour mill were to catch fire.

Fortunately the flour mill was saved, although two hours after Al had started his fire experiment, the barn was nothing but a smoldering pile of charred wood. In fact, the charred wood interested Al, who would have liked to have taken a closer look at it, but his father was angrier than he had ever seen him before, and Al dared not go near the barn. It was not long before the wrath of Samuel Edison came to bear upon his son. Tears ran down Al's cheeks as he tried to explain why he had lit the fire, but his father was in no mood to hear his excuses. Al felt his father grab the collar of his shirt and jerk him forward. Before he knew what was happening, Al was being half pulled and half led to the town square. There his father picked up a switch, and Al was forced to bend over.

"I hope this makes an impression on you and any other child who might be tempted to do such a stupid thing as light a fire in a barn," Al heard his father say as he felt the sting of the switch slamming against his buttocks. Over and over Samuel swung the switch as tears rolled down Al's face and dripped onto his shirt. But Al was not crying just because of the pain he was feeling on his backside. He was crying also because of the humiliation of being whipped in the middle of town while other children and their parents stood around watching.

Finally the punishment was over, and Samuel marched Al, his behind welted and stinging, back home.

Despite his public whipping for setting the barn ablaze, Al normally enjoyed a happy family life. He felt well loved, even though he wished his brother and sisters were a little closer to him in age. They were all a lot older than he. By his sixth birthday, his sister, Marion, was a twenty-three-year-old married woman; his brother, Pitt, was twenty-one years old; and his other sister, Harriet, was eighteen. Sometimes Al's mother told him about three other siblings: Carlile and Sam, who had died long before Al was born, and a sister, Eliza, who had died when Al was a baby. As the youngest in the family, Al adjusted to being alone a lot of the time.

Al had to endure one other whipping, though this time it was carried out in the privacy of his bedroom. The whipping occurred after Al had convinced the young girl next door to eat mashed worms. Al had been wondering whether eating worms was what made birds able to fly, and so he had convinced the girl to eat the worms to test his theory.

Apart from the worm theory and the incident with the barn, everything seemed to be going well for Al and his family and for the town of Milan. That's why it was a surprise to Al when he overheard his parents talking one evening in hushed tones. Al was standing in the kitchen garden, studying a ladybug's wings, when through the open window he heard his mother say, "Are you sure about this, Samuel?" Her voice had an unfamiliar sound to it—a sound of worry.

"Mark my words," Samuel Edison replied. "The people of Milan have made a huge mistake letting the railway bypass them. The future is in that railway, not the canal. There might be only three hundred miles of railway track in Ohio today, but one day all of the grain will be headed to the coast in freight trains, and we'll be left high and dry here, canal or no canal. It makes perfect sense. The canals are useless for five months because of the winter freeze. We were fools to turn down the offer of railroad tracks through town."

"What should we do?" Al heard his mother say in a voice barely above a whisper.

"I don't see anything for us but to move. Milan's golden age will be over in five years or less, and the shipyards will lie empty. Nothing will be able to compete with a train going thirty miles an hour. We have to get ahead of things, or we will be caught when the town starts losing money."

Al felt a surge of joy rush through his body at his father's words. Had he heard right? Was the family going to head west in one of the prairie schooners he used to love to watch as they passed through town? Or were they going to head east to the coast, where, his brother Pitt had told him, hundreds of ships sailed the Atlantic Ocean? Al did not know what to make of the conversation he had just over-heard, and he found it hard not to ask questions about it. But to do so would alert his parents to the fact that he had been eavesdropping on them.

A week after Al overheard his parents' conversation, Samuel Edison informed the family that they were moving away from Milan. But much to Al's disappointment, they would not be heading west or east but would be going 180 miles north to Port Huron, Michigan. "That's where the action will be," Al's father predicted. "The place is not much at the moment, but soon it's going to be connected with Detroit by rail, and that's the moment of opportunity."

And so the Edison family sold their house and the shingle mill and prepared for the move. Seven-year-old Al was disturbed when he realized that his big sister Marion would not be going north with them. She was staying on the farm outside of Milan with her husband, Homer Page. Despite their age difference, Al would miss her.

It was a beautiful spring day in 1854 when the Edison family packed up and left Milan for good. Al felt shy as he said good-bye to Marion. Homer ruffled Al's blond hair and said, "Now, whatever you do, don't go sitting on goose eggs!" Everyone laughed, and Al felt himself turning red. He had heard the story retold a hundred times and wondered whether he would ever outgrow it. As a three-year-old he had wondered what made an egg hatch. His mother had told him that it was the warmth of a mother bird sitting on it that caused the egg to hatch. One day, soon after Marion and Homer were married, Al decided to see whether the answer was right. He visited the barn, gathered up all the hen and goose eggs he could find, and built a nest for himself out of straw. He placed the eggs in the nest and then sat on them. Needless to say he ended up with egg all over his pants and in the process created an amusing story that was repeated at every family gathering.

Soon Al, Harriet, and Pitt and their parents were rolling along in a wagon that was taking them on the first leg of their journey ten miles south to Norwalk, where they would catch a train for Toledo. From Toledo they would take another wagon north to Detroit, Michigan, where they would board a steamer for the trip across Lake St. Clair and then up the river to Port Huron.

As the wagon carried Al away from the only home he had ever known, Al's mother told him stories of other family journeys. His favorite story was the one about his father fleeing from Canada.

Al's great-grandfather, John Edeson, had lived in New Jersey and had been a loyalist sympathizer throughout the Revolutionary War. Following the war he had refused to take the "Oath of Abjuration and Allegiance" to the newly formed United States. Eventually the Edeson family was forced to flee north to Nova Scotia, Canada, where they joined forty thousand other American loyalists who had also fled the United States. Upon their arrival in Canada, the family name was changed from Edeson to Edison.

The Edison family spent many years farming in windswept Nova Scotia. Eventually they headed west and settled in Ontario, where a small community called Vienna had sprung up. It was in Vienna that Al's father, Samuel, was born and where, on September 12, 1828, Samuel married Al's mother, Nancy Elliot, an American from New York State. Vienna was also where Al's older siblings, Marion, Pitt, Harriet, and Carlile were born.

In 1837, Samuel Edison was forced to flee from Canada to the United States or be hanged for treason. This was because he had taken part in the Mackenzie Rebellion. William Lyon Mackenzie had been the mayor of Toronto. Just as the American colonists had sixty years before, he had grown tired of the heavy hand of the British Crown in the daily affairs of Canada, and in a familiar cry he had objected to taxation without representation. A rebellion to overthrow the British authorities was fermented, and Al's father was drawn into it.

Samuel marched with a group of rebels to join the rebellion in Toronto, but the British militia easily quashed the rebellion, and the rebels were forced to flee. Nine members of Samuel Edison's rebel brigade from Vienna were caught and hanged for treason. Since the same fate awaited Samuel if he stayed in Canada, he fled south to the United States, with the militia in hot pursuit. Fortunately Samuel made it to safety in Fort Huron, Michigan, and eventually he made his way to Milan, Ohio.

Once settled in Milan, Samuel Edison made friends with Captain Alva Bradley, a shipowner from Vermilion, Ohio. It was Captain Bradley who had sailed across Lake Erie to Canada and picked up Nancy Edison and her four children and brought them back to Milan, where the Edison family was reunited. And it was Captain Bradley who had loaned Samuel Edison the money to start the shingle mill in Milan. When Al was born, he was named Thomas after his uncle in Canada and Alva after Captain Bradley.

Of course Al had heard the story of his father fleeing Canada many times before, but this time it seemed more real to him, now that the family was on the move again.

Soon, though, Al did not need his mother to distract him with stories to help pass the time. After boarding the train for Toledo in Norwalk, Al sat with his nose pressed against the carriage window. While his mother fretted that the train would derail, Al reveled in the excitement of going so fast. Fields and houses and people seemed to whiz by as the train rolled along.

The steamboat ride from Detroit to Port Huron was just as exciting. There were few Indians around Milan, but out on Lake St. Clair, Indians paddling in canoes seemed to be everywhere. Small Indian villages dotted the edges of the lake and on up the river. Al leaned out over the vessel's railing trying to catch a better view of them. It was all so exciting, and by the time the steamer arrived in Port Huron, Al was eager to see the big two-story house in the woods on the outskirts of town that was to become his new home.

Chapter 3

Port Huron

The locals call it the White House," Al's mother told him as the two of them stood outside looking up at the huge house. "It has six bedrooms upstairs, and I think you might like the one second from the end. See, it has the best view of Lake Huron."

Al squeezed his mother's hand, pleased that she knew exactly the bedroom he would like. The two of them explored the grounds of the house together. There was a carriage house, where most of the family's belongings were packed in boxes, a barn, an ice-house, and a woodshed. "And look," his mother said, as she led Al inside. "We even have an oven in the kitchen fireplace. I bet it will bake the best apple pies."

Al nodded. "I hope it's not too long till we find out."

Nancy Edison ruffled her son's hair. "In the morning you can help Pitt bring some boxes into the

25

house, and when I've unpacked my kitchen things, we'll find out."

The following morning, after a good night's sleep in his new bedroom, Al busied himself helping Pitt carry boxes into the house. He loved their new home in Port Huron. It was much bigger than the house in Milan, and he had not yet had a chance to explore the cellar or the orchard.

Before long all of the family's belongings had been lugged into the house and arranged. Now, with everything in order, it was time for the various members of the Edison family to find ways of making a living. Pitt became a partner in a livery stable in town and moved into a small house beside the stable, while Samuel Edison dabbled in a variety of money-making schemes. He ran a grocery store, sold timber from his new property, and turned the land into a productive farm. But best of all, he built a tower.

Al was amazed as his father's handiwork began to take shape. The one-hundred-foot-tall wooden observation tower was located right next to the house. From the top of the tower Al could see the St. Clair River, Lake Huron. and the seventy-four-foot-tall brick tower at Fort Gratiot that served as a lighthouse. His mother informed him that a lighthouse had stood on that spot since 1825, along with a military outpost to ensure the safe passage of vessels between Lake Huron and the St. Clair River.

Samuel Edison charged visitors twenty-five cents to climb to the top of his observation tower and peer through the telescope he had mounted there. Some of the townsfolk came regularly to take in the view, but Al was by far the most frequent visitor to the top of the tower. He loved to stand and feel the wind rush against his face and watch the various vessels that bobbed their way across Lake Huron.

Al's happy pursuits came to an abrupt end one day when he got sick. The illness started out with a headache and chills, and then a bright red rash spread quickly over his body. Samuel and Nancy Edison called the doctor, who pronounced the dreaded diagnosis: their youngest son had scarlet fever.

Scarlet fever was a serious illness. More children Al's age died from the disease than made a recovery, but Al did not know that at the time. All he knew was that his body itched and his bones ached. His mother nursed him around the clock, keeping his body cool with vinegar-soaked towels and coaxing him to sip water. Thankfully, under his mother's care, Al began to show signs of recovery, though he complained about pain in his ears. Eventually he did get better, but he was left with impaired hearing and a weak chest, which meant that he seemed to catch every cold and influenza bug that came his way.

Because of the weakened state of Al's health, his parents did not send him to school until he was eight and a half years old. Since Port Huron had no public school at that time, Al was enrolled in the Family School for Boys and Girls, a Presbyterian school run by the local minister, the Reverend George Engle. Nancy Edison was particularly pleased that it was a Presbyterian school. Although her father had been a Baptist minister in New York State, she had converted to Presbyterianism. She took Al to church with her every Sunday, though Samuel refused to go with his wife and son.

The Reverend Engle and his niece, who was the school's head teacher, both believed that children learned best by reciting facts, saying little, and offering total obedience to their teacher. This was a disastrous formula for Al Edison, who had grown up with older siblings and was used to being treated as an equal around adults. Worse, Al had to ask questions about everything around him, and the Reverend Engle and his niece had no tolerance for questions. If Al diligently completed his lessons, they told him, he would find all the answers he sought. Al didn't believe them for one minute.

Al soon grew very bored with school. His mind wandered in class, he forgot his homework, and he found it hard to hear his teacher, since he was made to sit with the slow learners at the back of the classroom. He should have been placed at the front so that he could lip-read. When Al did not finish his class work on time, he was forced to write over and over (up to one hundred times) such lines as "The idle boy is almost invariably poor and miserable; the industrious boy is happy and prosperous." The repetition of writing such statements was supposed to spur him on to work harder, but for Al it had the opposite effect.

There was no doubt in anyone's mind that Al was miserable at school. There was some question, however, as to why he was so miserable. Al had the impression that his father did not think he was very smart, and one day he was startled to learn that this was definitely what the Reverend Engle believed. He made this discovery one lunch hour when an inspector came to check on the students' progress at the Family School for Boys and Girls. During the visit Al overheard the Reverend Engle tell the inspector that he thought Al was addled.

ADDLED! Al wanted to scream. *Addled* meant muddled in his thinking and stupid. It was too much for Al, who grabbed his lunch pail and ran all the way home. By the time he got there, he had been crying so hard that his eyes were burning.

"What's the matter, Al?" his mother asked as he rushed through the front door.

"The teacher called me addled, and I'm not addled, am I?" he replied.

Nancy turned bright red. "Addled? Addled? You? Addled? The man must be mad! Of course you're not addled. I bet you are the brightest boy in the class. He doesn't know what he's talking about. Wait here."

Al waited in the doorway while his mother disappeared and then returned a few minutes later carrying her shawl and purse. "We will get to the bottom of this. You deserve an apology," Nancy said, sweeping past Al and out the door. Al followed, and the two of them walked briskly back to the school. Al's mother had lost none of her indignation by the time she got there. She stormed into the classroom. "Mr. Engle, I need to speak to you now," she said forthrightly.

Al felt like smiling. He had seldom seen his mother so angry, and it was good to know that she was on his side.

"I believe you think my son is addled," she began. "Is that right?"

The Reverend Engle looked embarrassed at first but finally spoke up. "Well, Mrs. Edison, there is no denying that he has the lowest grades in the class, and whenever I ask him to recite something, he cannot do it correctly."

"Humph," Mrs. Edison replied. "I was a schoolteacher myself before I got married, and I can assure you I know a bright boy when I see one. My son is the brightest boy I've ever seen. If he isn't learning anything in this classroom, it is not because he's addled. It's because you don't know how to teach."

The Reverend Engle glared at them both, and his ears turned bright red.

"Furthermore, before I allow my son to return here, I demand that you apologize to him," Nancy Edison demanded.

"I certainly will not, ma'am. You might think your son is a genius, but I don't see any evidence of it, and I will not apologize to a boy," the Reverend Engle snapped.

Al felt a tug on his arm. "Then, Mr. Engle, you will not see my son again in this class. I shall teach him myself." With that, Al's mother swung her son around and the two of them marched out the door.

As they walked home in silence, Al could hardly take in what had just happened. He was free from school; he would never have to go back there and learn lists of boring spelling words and tedious history dates. He was so excited he wanted to skip, not walk.

The next day, Al's homeschooling began. His mother had to fit his lessons in between her housework and cooking chores, but Al did not need a lot of guidance. He soon learned to read, first simple readers and then anything he could get his hands on. Before long his mother was buying him copies of Thomas Paine's *Age of Reason,* David Hume's *History of England,* and Edward Gibbon's *Decline and Fall of the Roman Empire.* These were not the usual books a nine-year-old would read, but Al devoured them. He would often climb to the top of the observation tower and read to himself high above the treetops. This new venue for learning certainly beat sitting in a cramped classroom reciting endless phrases.

One day Al's mother sent away for a book that was to immediately become Al's favorite volume. The book by R. G. Parker was called *A School Compendium of Natural and Experimental Philosophy,* and from the moment Al opened it, he could not put it down. The book was a compilation of the known scientific facts on all manner of subjects, such as mechanics and the laws of motion, electricity, optics, magnetism, astronomy, and chemistry. Within the pages of the book were also listed hundreds of different experiments that could be carried out at home or in the classroom. Al soon found himself carrying out many of the experiments. In the process he built two machines for generating electricity: one using friction to generate the current and the other using magnetism. Soon the shelves in his bedroom were lined with scraps of metal and wire and odd-shaped jars, bottles, and tins containing an assortment of chemicals and substances Al bought with his pocket money.

It was not long, though, before Al's mother objected to the strong chemical smells that emanated from Al's bedroom, not to mention the spilled acid that ate away at the floorboards. Nancy banished her son's experimenting activities to the basement, where Al set up a lab among baskets of potatoes, carrots, and onions, and jars of his mother's canned fruits and vegetables.

At nine years of age, Thomas Alva Edison had found his passion in life. He spent hundreds of hours in his bedroom reading or in the basement carrying out experiments. He did this partly because he liked time alone to think and partly because he and his parents soon became the only occupants in the large house. In 1856 Al's sister Harriet married Samuel Bailley, a nearby farmer, and his brother Pitt married Nellie Holihan.

Besides reading his science books, Al liked to scan the local newspapers for any scientific information he could find. In 1856 he read about how Englishman Henry Bessemer had invented and patented a process for converting iron into steel that involved blasts of air being blown through the molten iron, which oxidized and removed unwanted impurities from the metal.

That same year Al also read about a man named David Hughes, a music professor in Kentucky who had invented a printing telegraph that used a vibrating spring tuned to a specific pitch to synchronize the sending and receiving of telegrams using a code invented by him. News of Hughes's device called to mind another inventor—Samuel Morse—whom Al had read about in *A School Compendium of Natural and Experimental Philosophy.* Morse had also invented a telegraph machine and a code for sending messages. Morse's system used electromagnetic pulses of either long or short duration tapped out by a telegraph operator on a telegraph key and sent over wires to a telegraph. The receiver turned the pulses back into a series of long and short taps or dots and dashes that another telegraph operator could decode and then write down the message being sent. Morse's code was reproduced in the *Compendium,* and Al set to learning it. Soon he was tapping out his name with his finger on the tabletop:

A—dot dash
L—dot dash dot dot
E—dot
D—dash dot dot
I—dot dot
S—dot dot dot
O—dash dash dash
N—dash dot

Once he had learned Morse code, Al decided it was time to set up his own telegraph line from his house through the woods to a friend's house nearby. For the line he used a narrow strand of wire that was usually reserved for holding chimneys in place, and from a science magazine he figured out how to construct a key. Soon he was tapping out messages to his friend. Of course the signal sometimes became degraded on its way down the line, and then Al's friend would yell at Al from his bedroom window, "What did you say?"

In 1858, when Al was eleven years old, every newspaper in the country bore the same headline: "First Trans-Atlantic Telegraph Cable Completed." It was a fantastic achievement, and soon afterward Queen Victoria of England and President Buchanan of the United States exchanged messages via telegraph. For the first time in the history of the world, a person on one continent could communicate directly with a person on another continent without either person having to travel there. Now news could pass from Europe to North America almost instantaneously, instead of taking the six weeks it normally required to cross the Atlantic Ocean by ship.

Closer to home, the debate as to whether or not it should be legal to keep slaves was heating up. A year later, in 1859, the abolitionist John Brown led a raid on the government arsenal at Harpers Ferry, Virginia, in the hope of capturing weapons to be used in a revolt to free the slaves. Brown was captured and hanged, but the argument about slavery raged on.

It was also in 1859, just after Al turned twelve years old, that he and his father caught a train back to Milan, Ohio, to visit his sister Marion. The Grand Trunk Railroad of Canada had built a railway line from Port Huron to Detroit. The trip provided Al with a chance to experience firsthand riding on the new line. The railway was an important link to Detroit, from where you were able to change trains and travel all the way to New York or Chicago. At Port Huron the rail system linked to the railroad in Canada. Train cars were ferried across the St. Clair River between Port Huron and Sarnia in Ontario, Canada, making it possible to travel vast distances across the North American landscape by train.

As the train lumbered along on its way to Detroit, Al was particularly interested in watching the "candy butch" work. The candy butch was a young man, probably only a year or two older than Al. The candy butch's job was to walk up and down the aisles of the carriages selling newspapers, magazines, candies, and fruit from a well-stocked basket. The young man would stop to laugh and joke with the passengers as he went along, and he would take time at the end of each carriage to read one of the newspapers he was selling. That way he would have more information to discuss with the next group of passengers.

By the time Al had returned home to Port Huron from Milan, he was determined to become a candy butch on the new Detroit–Port Huron train.

Candy Butch

As it turned out, Al did not have a particularly difficult time convincing his father that he should
go to work on the railroad. Several of his father's
business deals had fallen through lately, and the
family needed extra income. Al's mother proved more
difficult to convince. She did not know exactly what
Al's future would look like, but in her mind it did
not involve selling candy on a train. She also worried about the long stopover her son would have to
spend in Detroit. The train left Port Huron at seven
in the morning and arrived in Detroit about 10:00
AM, where it stayed in the train yard all day until
6:00 PM, when it set out on the return journey to
Port Huron. The journey each way from Detroit to
Port Huron was sixty-three miles, and the trip took
about three hours, with various stops along the way,
to cover that distance.

Not only would this schedule make it a very long day for a twelve-year-old boy, but also, as Nancy Edison pointed out, it involved spending a lot of time in a big city where there was crime and violence, with brawls often erupting in saloons and spilling into the streets. Nancy fretted that these were things a country boy would not know how to handle.

Finally Al appealed to his mother's schoolteacher side. He told his mother that during his stopovers in Detroit he intended to enroll in the Detroit Young Men's Society and read his way through its entire library of books. With this promise, Nancy relented, and Samuel took his son into Port Huron to talk to the train's conductor, a Scotsman named Alexander Stephenson. Mr. Stephenson was delighted to give Al a job, because in all his business dealings with Mr. Edison he had found him to be an honest man.

The next morning Al hitched up the horse to the buggy for the trip into Port Huron. At six o'clock when he left, it was still dark. Al whipped the horse to make the animal go faster as they passed the Fort Gratiot Cemetery, where three hundred soldiers who had died during the cholera epidemic of 1832 lay buried. Al was frightened by the thought of all those graves, and he held his breath as he passed by them.

Once he arrived in Port Huron, Al delivered the horse and buggy to the livery stable for the day and reported to Alexander Stephenson.

"The job's na difficult," Mr. Stephenson told Al in his Scottish brogue. "Ye should pick it up quickly. Ye will'na have anything on ye to sell this morning, but once ye get to Detroit ye should buy up candy, peanuts, cigars, fruit—anything ye thinks ye can sell—and o' course newspapers. Ye arrange them in this basket and sell them to passengers on the way back here. Buy ye self enough of everything so that tomorrow ye will have merchandize ta sell on your way to Detroit. Any questions?"

Al nodded. "Where do I go when I'm not selling things?"

"Och, yes, I forgot ta mention that ta ye," Mr. Stephenson said, scratching his head. "There be always room for yer things in the baggage car. Ye'll be sharing it with me, and there be a trunk in there where ye can put the things you do nay want ta take home at night. Mind you, put the lid down though. Rats play havoc around here at night."

Al loved the job from the start. The carriages were constantly filling and emptying with interesting people. And since there were no first-class seats, everyone sat together—wealthy travelers from the East, young country mothers and their children, and railroad officials checking the Grand Trunk line and doing business along the way.

The train journey itself could be hazardous as the train sped along, sometimes at over twenty miles per hour. The rail system relied on a series of flagmen to make sure that two trains were not going in opposite directions on the same track. But even with this precaution, there was always the chance of a full-on collision with another train. Derailment, though, was a much more common hazard. Animals wandered onto the track, and debris littered it, especially after a storm. Either of these could cause the train's wheels to jump the rails. Sometimes the engineer would take a curve too fast, causing carriages to overbalance and roll off the tracks. When this happened, the most dangerous object in a carriage was the wood-burning stove, which kept the passengers warm in winter. The stove would become an airborne fireball.

Al didn't mind these risks, though. In fact, they added to the sense of adventure he felt. Al also loved the challenge of seeing how much he could sell in a day. He soon worked out the best order in which to offer his wares. First he would offer the passengers salty foods—peanuts and egg sandwiches. After they had eaten these, the passengers would grow thirsty from the salt, and Al would then sell them juices and apples. Then he'd offer magazines, books, and newspapers for sale for the people to read on the remainder of the journey.

Although Al normally found it difficult to hear, the low rumbling of the train wheels against the steel rails did not make hearing any harder for him. In fact, it seemed to make it easier because the passengers were forced to speak louder to be heard above the noise, and Al could hear them easily.

Candy butches were well known for pushing their wares on passengers, and Al proudly posted a cartoon in the baggage car. The cartoon showed a candy butch asking a passenger, "Rock candy, rock candy, sir?" and the passenger replying, "No, no, go away. I don't have any teeth." To this the candy butch replies, "Gum drops, sir?" Al thought the cartoon was very funny. It reminded him that every passenger was a potential customer if he could just find the thing he or she needed at that moment.

Al lost no time in joining the Detroit Young Men's Society so that he could use its library. He had promised his mother that he would read every book there, and he set to work, starting with Thomas Burton's *Anatomy of Melancholy*. This book, first published in 1621, covered all sorts of topics, including medicine, astronomy, philosophy, literature, the arts, politics, and nature.

In Detroit Al also loved to stroll through the streets. Detroit was one of America's fast-growing industrial cities, with a population of about fifty thousand people. The city was a mishmash of elegant buildings standing alongside tumbledown shacks, and people of various nationalities spilled into the streets. On street corners it was not uncommon for Al to see men and women dressed in the latest fashions from the East standing beside others dressed in nothing more than rags. Beggars and prostitutes also plied the streets, and as Al's mother had worried, brawls were commonplace, though Al was careful to stay well away from them. Al loved to walk along the Detroit waterfront, where sailing ships, steamers, and barges were busily being loaded and unloaded. He would wonder where the vessels were going next and what their cargo was going to be used for.

Each afternoon Al walked to the *Detroit Free Press* office to collect the newspapers he would sell on the trip north to Port Huron. On his visits to the newspaper office, he loved to watch the printers as they set row upon row of metal type onto plates that would be placed on the printing press to print the next edition of the paper.

Al would also scan the headlines of the newspaper and read the main articles on the front page, both to satisfy his own curiosity and to look for selling points that he could use to entice the passengers on the train to buy a paper from him. Throughout 1860 the headlines were all about the growing tensions between the northern and southern states over the issue of slavery. In late 1860 the headlines declared that Abraham Lincoln from Illinois had been elected president. Shortly afterward, on December 20, 1860, the headlines told of South Carolina's decision to secede from the Union over the issue of the ownership of slaves. This was followed on February 1, 1861, by a headline stating that Alabama, Mississippi, Florida, Georgia, Louisiana, and Texas had followed South Carolina's lead and had also seceded from the Union. And then three days later, Al read that these states had banded together to form the Confederate States of America and had chosen Jefferson Davis to be their president.

Things were not going well for the country, Al had to admit, though it was hard to tell that much had changed in this isolated corner of the Midwest. Still, talk of war between the North and the South was everywhere. The newspapers reported that politicians in Washington, D.C., were desperately trying to find a compromise, but none was forthcoming. On April 12, 1861, before Union ships could resupply the Union garrison at Fort Sumter, located in the mouth of the harbor in Charleston, South Carolina, batteries of Confederate cannons opened fire on the fort. The next day the Fort Sumter garrison surrendered to the Confederates—the Civil War had begun. Soon after the fall of Fort Sumter, the headlines told of how Virginia, North Carolina, Arkansas, and Tennessee had also seceded from the Union and had joined the Confederacy. Soon after that, another headline revealed that General Robert E. Lee had resigned from the Union army rather than lead federal troops against his native Virginia.

As 1861 progressed, the news was not good for the Union army. It seemed the army could not win against Confederate forces, and the headlines told of Union defeats at Bull Run and Ball's Bluff, Virginia. Young men from Michigan were soon being called up to serve in the Union army. As a result, many train travelers clamored to buy newspapers to read the latest developments in the war and assure themselves that their sons and husbands and brothers were safe.

At the Detroit Young Men's Society, Al had changed his goal. He had originally intended to read all the books in the library, but after attempting several volumes that were so dry and boring that they were virtually unreadable, he decided to read only those books that interested him. Soon he had read every science book in the place.

Al then began looking around for some other interesting activity to fill his time in Detroit. He wished he had space somewhere to set up a laboratory and conduct experiments instead of having to wait for Sundays, his only day off, to work in his basement lab at home. Then a thought struck him.

The baggage car was always half empty. Why not set up a lab there? That way he could experiment to his heart's content while waiting for the return trip to Port Huron.

Al got permission from Alexander Stevenson to set up a lab, and he began to gather the chemicals and other bits and pieces he needed. Soon jars and bottles with various chemicals and liquids were lined up on shelves in the baggage car. Al constructed the shelves in such a way that the bottles and jars would not break loose and fall to the floor as the train rumbled along. He used his hours in Detroit conducting experiments. He particularly enjoyed experiments with chemicals and electricity, and he also built a rough but functional telegraph key.

Al was not always as careful with his chemicals as he should have been, and one time he neglected to replace the water that had evaporated from a jar of phosphorous that stood on his shelf. As a result, the jar of phosphorous caught fire and fell to the floor of the baggage car. Soon the floor of the car was ablaze, and Al could not put the fire out by himself. Fortunately Mr. Stevenson arrived in time to help extinguish the flames before the whole car burned.

When the flames had died down, the conductor turned his rage on Al. In fact, Al had never before seen Alexander Stevenson so angry. The man's puffy face turned bright red as he scolded Al for his carelessness. Al wondered if the now-bulging veins in the conductor's neck might burst. He watched helplessly as Mr. Stevenson gathered up all of the chemicals and pieces of apparatus and tossed them from the baggage car onto the side of the railroad track. And then in his Scottish brogue, Mr. Stevenson forbade Al from ever bringing chemicals onto the train again.

This was Al's second disaster with fire. And while he had not enjoyed being on the receiving end of Alexander Stevenson's wrath, Al was glad that the conductor had not publicly scolded and humiliated him as his father had done when he had set the barn ablaze.

On the afternoon of April 7, 1862, not too long after he had set the baggage car on fire, Al made his usual afternoon trek to the *Detroit Free Press* office to collect his supply of newspapers for the return trip to Port Huron. To his surprise he had to push through a large crowd gathered at the office. When he saw the headline, Al knew why the crowd was there. Flashed across the front page of the day's edition of the newspaper was the story of the Battle of Shiloh that had taken place in southern Tennessee.

Confederate forces had staged a surprise attack on General Ulysses S. Grant's Union army the day before while they were encamped near a church named Shiloh. The surprise and the force of the attack had left Grant's troops reeling, and the men had been forced to retreat to the Tennessee River. However, during the night, over twenty-two thousand soldiers had reinforced the Union lines. At first light the reinforced Union army had struck back, eventually forcing a Confederate retreat and allowing General Grant to capture the railhead at Corinth, just across the border in Mississippi, cutting off the Confederate's main east-west supply line.

According to the report, seventy thousand men had fought in the battle, and over twenty-three thousand of them had been killed. This was the bloodiest battle of the Civil War so far, and Al could understand why people were clamoring for news of the battle. Many of them had sons and husbands and brothers who had fought in it. That was when inspiration struck Al. Normally he would have collected one hundred copies of the newspaper to sell on the train, but with this news he decided he needed more. He counted up his money. He had enough to purchase three hundred copies of the paper, but decided that he needed even more than that. He convinced the newspaper's editor to let him have another seven hundred copies of the paper on consignment. Reluctantly the editor agreed, and Al soon had one thousand copies of the day's edition of the *Detroit Free Press* loaded onto the train.

Al then set the second phase of his plan in motion. By now, telegraph wires stretched alongside the railway tracks all the way to Port Huron. The main function of this telegraph system was to communicate with the various stations along the line as to which trains were on which tracks, thus reducing the chance of accidents. Fascinated as he was with the telegraph, Al had made friends with the various telegraph operators along the line. Now he decided that it was time to put the telegraph to another use. He convinced the telegraph operator in Detroit to telegraph the headline from the day's newspaper ahead to all the stations along the railroad line and have the telegraph operators at those stations post the headline on a blackboard for all to read.

Al's plan worked like a charm. When the train stopped at the first station on the journey north, Utica, Al sold thirty-five copies of the newspaper rather than the two he normally sold there. At the next station, Mount Clemens, people clamored for a copy of the paper to read news of the Battle of Shiloh. This time Al upped the price to ten cents each rather than the normal five-cent cost.

By the time the train reached Port Huron, Al was selling the newspapers for a quarter apiece. Even at this price, the last of his thousand copies of the newspaper were quickly snapped up by the residents of Port Huron.

Al made his way home that night with more money in his pocket than he had ever had before, and with a scheme to make even more. A plan was forming in his mind to publish his own newspaper, not a paper like the *Detroit Free Press* that carried lots of national news, but a local newspaper that told about events along the railway line between Detroit and Port Huron. The paper would also publish the train timetables.

Al's first job in making this venture a reality was convincing Alexander Stevenson that setting up a printing press in the repaired baggage car was a totally safe proposition. Al assured the conductor that there was no danger whatsoever of the printing press catching fire or exploding. Reluctantly Mr. Stevenson finally agreed to the scheme.

Al's next job was finding a small printing press and installing it in the baggage car. Al found a small, disused printing press in Detroit and purchased it cheaply. He then convinced the printers at the

Detroit Free Press to give him three hundred pounds of disused metal type, and Al was in business. He called his newspaper the *Weekly Herald* and sold it to passengers for eight cents a copy. The paper was chockful of local news and gossip. It reported the births and deaths of people who lived along the rail-road. Al also published the names of local men serving in the Union army, as well as any pieces of news about the war he was able to get his hands on. All in all, he was very happy with his accomplishment, though setting the type for each edition was no easy task, and he doubted that he wanted to be a newspaper publisher all his life. But he did dream about becoming an engine driver.

One day, when he was fifteen years old, Al got the opportunity to try his hand at driving an engine. He convinced the engineer to let him ride in the engine cab with him on one of the trips south to Detroit. He busied himself firing logs into the fire-box of the engine and polishing the brass fittings while the engineer and fireman watched with smiles on their faces.

The engineer had been out late the night before, and when the engine pulled into a station to pick up passengers, he decided to retire to the baggage car for a nap, leaving the fireman and Al to run the engine. As the train rolled along, Al noticed that the fireman was also beginning to doze, and he offered to take over running the engine. The fireman took up Al's offer, and soon Al was in control of the engine. Because Al knew that it was important to make sure that the water level in the boiler did not get too low, he kept pumping water into the boiler. He was unaware, however, that he was letting too much water into the boiler. The excess water was being blown out the smokestack, where it mixed with soot, forming a black mud that splattered all over the engine—and all over Al.

Al had also observed that every so often the fireman would go out to the cowcatcher, where he would open the oil cup to the engine's steam chest and pour more oil in. Al decided that he should do this as well. Unfortunately, when he opened the oil cup, steam burst out, scalding his hands and plastering his already muddied face and hands with hot oil. Al had failed to notice that the engineer always shut off the steam before the fireman opened the oil cup.

Al finally managed to get the engine to its destination, though he arrived in Detroit looking more like a chimney sweep than an engineer, and his blistered hands ached. He then decided that being an engineer was not for him.

By the fall of 1862, Al was feeling bored with life. He had been up and down the railway line between Port Huron and Detroit so many times that he could tell every curve with his eyes shut. He'd read every book in the Detroit Young Men's Society library that interested him. He had mastered the art of being a candy butch, tried his hand at being a newspaper publisher, and ruled out being a train driver. He was beginning to wonder what he should do next when a three-year-old boy changed the course of his life.

Chapter 5

A Roving Telegraph Operator

One morning on his journey south, Al decided to stay at the Mount Clemens railroad station. He allowed two of his friends, Jim Clancy and Tommy Sutherland, to take over his candy-butching duties for the rest of the trip to Detroit. He would rejoin the train as it headed north again in the early evening. James MacKenzie, the stationmaster at Mount Clemens, allowed Al to watch him transmit and receive Morse-coded telegraphic messages. Al was always amazed at the speed with which a telegraph operator could tap out letters in code.

During the course of the day, Al took a break from watching Mr. MacKenzie. He decided to stretch his legs by strolling along the station platform. As he was just about to turn and head back inside the station, he heard the brakeman yell, "Get out of the way!"

Al immediately swung around and took in the scene. The brakeman was on top of a freight car rolling down the track, while Jimmie, the station-master's three-year-old son, sat on the track as the freight car sped toward him. There was no time to waste! In an instant Al leaped from the station plat-form, darted over, and plucked Jimmie from the tracks. Seconds later, metal wheels screeched past the spot where the boy had been sitting.

Mrs. MacKenzie, having witnessed the rescue from a window in the station, came running out screaming. She took her son in her arms and thanked Al profusely. Mr. MacKenzie arrived on the scene moments later. He was equally grateful. "We owe you our son's life. What can we do for you?" he asked.

Al smiled. He knew exactly what James MacKenzie could do for him. "You could train me as a telegraph operator," he replied.

Mr. MacKenzie patted Al on the back. "You can start tomorrow, lad," he said.

Within three months Al was good enough at transmitting and receiving telegraph messages to look for a job of his own. Because he already knew Morse code and had an understanding of the scien-tific principles that made telegraphy possible, he made fast progress in learning the art of being a telegraph operator. In addition he had already con-structed a simple telegraph key in the course of his experiments. In fact, he had spent most of his three months of training learning the shorthand way to word messages, making them faster to tap out and send by Morse code.

Just as Al was becoming a competent telegraph operator, a job opened up for him at the Western Union telegraph office in downtown Port Huron. The office was located in Micah Walker's jewelry store, though in truth the store sold a little bit of just about everything: clocks, watches, cutlery, gold, silver, china, rifles, musical instruments, sheet music, schoolbooks, stationery, pens and pencils, technical manuals, and scientific magazines, which Al was allowed to read during downtime in telegraph transmissions.

Things went well for Al in his new job until he found he had too much spare time. After reading most of the scientific magazines, Al looked about for something else to fill his time. He took to conducting experiments in the back room of the store. Alas, this met with a fate similar to that of his experiments on the boxcar. During one experiment, Al mixed the wrong combination of chemicals together, which caused an explosion. Luckily the explosion was not big enough to destroy the store, but it was big enough to get Al fired. And as Al quickly found out, his reputation had preceded him throughout the region. Despite the demand for telegraph operators caused by the Civil War, Al was unable to find another job,

About this time, tragedy struck the Edison family. Harriet, Al's recently widowed sister, died during childbirth, along with the baby. Al's mother took the news particularly hard and became nervous and withdrawn. She might have recovered, but things got worse for the family. The Union army needed more quarters for troops near Fort Gratiot, and they commandeered the Edison house, evicting the family from it. The family moved into a smaller house on Cherry Street in Port Huron. Not long after the army took over the Edison home, a careless soldier accidentally set the place on fire, and the house burned to the ground. The loss of the lovely home sent Nancy Edison into an even deeper despair.

Eventually James MacKenzie used his influence and secured Al a job as a telegraph operator for the Grand Trunk Railroad at Stratford Junction, Ontario, Canada. Al was glad to leave the depressing atmosphere that surrounded him at home. At sixteen and a half years of age he decided to do his best to be a diligent and attentive employee for his new employer. He packed his belongings, crossed the St. Clair River, and caught a train headed toward Toronto. The seventy-five-mile ride took Al northeast to Stratford Junction, a pioneer town of thirty-five thousand residents located at the junction of the Grand Trunk Railroad's Toronto–Sarnia line and the Buffalo–Goderich Harbor line. Upon arrival in Stratford Junction, Al found a local boardinghouse and made arrangements with the landlady to stay there. Then he headed to the telegraph office to learn what his duties were going to be.

Throughout his life to this point, Al had always been called Al or Little Al by his family, but now, in a bold move to help him feel more like a man, Al decided to use his first name, Thomas—or Tom for short.

Tom soon spotted his new office—a large wooden crate that had once held dry goods and was now turned on its side and outfitted with a telegraph table.

He learned that all the trains traveling along the two lines stopped at Stratford Junction for about half an hour to take on coal and water. Of course, with two railway lines crossing as they did, the chance for a collision was great.

Tom's job involved sending information to and receiving information from other telegraph operators along the railroad lines as to which train was on which line and when to expect it at Stratford Junction. Before a train could cross the other rail line, it had to come to a complete stop. This was signaled to the train's engineer by the use of a semaphore flag signaling "Danger." When Tom received word that no train was coming on the other line, his job was to change the semaphore flag from "Danger" to "Caution." This signaled the engineer that it was safe for his train to cross the other line and proceed on into the railway station.

Tom would have found the job engaging, except for one thing: he worked the twelve-hour night shift, and during that time only one train in each direction passed through Stratford Junction. It was only a matter of time before Tom got bored and drifted back into his old habits. This time, though, he did not turn to chemistry experiments but to something that would help him get some rest during his long shift. Part of Tom's job was to send a Morse code message saying "6" down the line every half hour. All operators did this to assure their boss that they were awake and on the job. As far as Tom was concerned, the only thing between him and a good sleep was that number 6, so he tinkered with a clock and rigged it to the telegraph line so that it would automatically send the number 6 in Morse code every half hour.

This system worked well. Tom made sure he was always awake at the time the night trains were due to pass through Stratford Junction. But on the night of December 11, 1863, things went horribly wrong. The 11:15 PM freight train was approaching Stratford Junction from the west on the Buffalo–Goderich Harbor line, and the track had been switched to move the train onto a side track while it stopped to take on coal and water. At the same time a train was approaching from the east on the Toronto–Sarnia line.

Suddenly Tom remembered that he had forgotten to change the semaphore flag from "Caution" to "Danger" for the engineer of the train on the Toronto–Sarnia line. He grabbed a lantern and ran as fast as he could to change the flag, but he was too late. Upon seeing the "Caution" flag, the engineer had proceeded toward the station. But when his engine hit the switch that was set for the other train, it jumped the track, followed by the coal tender and the first boxcar. Fortunately no one was hurt in the accident, and the damage to the train and the track was minimal. But W. J. Spicer, manager of the Grand Trunk Railroad, was not impressed. He summoned Tom and the supervising agent of the station at Stratford Junction to company headquarters in Toronto to account for their actions.

Mr. Spicer was not satisfied with either Tom's or the station supervisor's explanation as to how and why the accident had occurred. He threatened to have both men charged with negligence and sent to jail, but before he could follow through on this, the meeting was interrupted by the arrival of some important English visitors who had an appointment to see W. J. Spicer. While the railroad manager met with the English visitors, Tom and the station supervisor were shown to an outer office to wait.

For his part, Tom decided that he did not want to spend time in a Canadian jail, so he slipped out of the headquarters building. Despite the fact that he was still owed twenty-eight dollars in wages, he hopped a train headed for Sarnia, located in Canada across the mouth of the St. Clair River from Port Huron. When he reached Sarnia, Tom trudged across the frozen river to Port Huron and back into the United States. Like his father before him, Tom Edison fled to the United States to avoid the punishment for his actions in Canada. His days of working for the Grand Trunk Railroad were over.

This time Tom did not even bother to go home. Instead he made his way straight from Port Huron to Toledo, Ohio, where he heard that the ever-expanding Western Union was hiring workers. He had no trouble getting a job and was assigned as a night operator in Adrian, Michigan, thirty-five miles northwest of Toledo. There he met and lived with a like-minded young man named Ezra Gilliland. Ezra was nineteen years old, and had been an apprentice gunsmith before the telegraph bug bit him. Ezra's father's cousin, Ezra Cornell, was a well-connected executive with the Michigan Southern Telegraph

Company, which was now part of the Western Union Company. He provided Tom and Ezra with some old telegraph equipment to experiment with.

Tom and Ezra spent hours tinkering with the equipment, even setting up a small workshop together, but the venture was short-lived. Tom got into an argument with his supervisor, and he was fired yet again. He was then hired by the Pittsburgh, Fort Wayne, and Chicago Railroad and was stationed in Fort Wayne, Indiana, as a telegraph operator. After working at this job for two months, Tom received word from Ezra Gilliland, who had moved to Cincinnati, Ohio, that there was an opening in the telegraph office in Indianapolis, Indiana.

Tom quickly caught a train to Indianapolis, where he was hired as a "plug," the lowest grade of telegraph operator, with a salary of seventy-five dollars a month. This was not a lot of money, but Tom was glad to have the job. On average Tom was competent at sending and receiving about fifteen words per minute. If he could improve this rate to about thirty words per minute, he would be able to receive a fifty percent pay increase. Tom set about trying to figure out a smart way to get faster at sending and receiving telegrams.

Tom found two old Morse code embossing registers lying around the office in Indianapolis. These old devices had been used in the days before operators had learned to decode messages from the clicking of the telegraph key. Essentially the register received the incoming message and recorded it as a series of embossed dots and dashes on a strip of paper, which an operator then used to decode the message. Tom began to tinker with the devices. He linked them together with a clockwork mechanism attached between the two registers. An incoming message could then be recorded onto the strip of paper, which in turn would be fed through the second register, which was rigged to a lever to produce the clicking sound of the telegraph key. The clockwork mechanism was implemented to slow down the speed at which the paper strip was fed through the second register, allowing an operator to decode and write down the message.

The device worked perfectly, and Tom and another plug, Ed Parmalee, began spending their evenings practicing decoding and writing down messages using it. While one of them kept watch over the clockwork mechanism to make sure that the two registers remained synchronized, the other decoded and wrote down the message, or took copy, as it was known to the telegraph operators. When they both became proficient taking copy at a certain speed, they adjusted the clockwork mechanism to speed up the second register, thus causing them to have to take copy faster. This approach worked perfectly, and soon Tom and Ed had greatly increased both their copy-taking speed and their income.

With the success of his device, Tom began thinking about other things it could be used for. In a flash he came up with a wonderful application. In 1864 a message could be transmitted over the wires for only about two hundred miles before its signal became too weak. As a result, if a message was to cover a distance of more than two hundred miles, it would have to be taken off the wire by a telegraph operator who would then retransmit it. Thinking about this problem, Tom wondered whether he could rig up a similar device using two registers, with the second register working a key to automatically retransmit the message and thus restore its signal strength. That way no human being would need to be involved in the process. Such telegraphic repeaters could be strategically placed along the wires so that a message could cover hundreds of miles without human intervention.

Tom and Ed began working on the idea night and day until they thought they had a device that would work. Satisfied with their effort, they lugged the repeater down to Union Station to try it out. Unfortunately, it malfunctioned, and Tom became so frustrated that he hurled the machine to the ground and walked away. Ed, though, was a calm and patient man, and he picked up the broken pieces of the repeater and took them back to their workshop to improve on the device. Before long Tom was back in their little workshop too, and eventually the two men got the repeater to work as it was supposed to. Before long they had hooked up repeaters along the Pittsburgh–St. Louis line so that it was possible to send a message from one city to the other without the need for a human being to transcribe and then retransmit it.

It should have been a moment of triumph for Tom, but it was not. Tom had skipped so many hours of work getting the device up and running that his boss had lost all patience with him and fired him. Instead of being patted on the back for inventing such a time-saving device, Tom found himself on the move again in search of another job. This time he made his way to Cincinnati, where Ezra Gilliland was living and working. With just fifty cents in his pocket, Tom hoped that Ezra's optimism was warranted and that good jobs were available for him in Cincinnati. Tom arrived in the city in February 1865, just in time for his eighteenth birthday. He got a job as a telegraph operator in Cincinnati and moved in with Ezra.

By March 1865, the Civil War was winding down. The Confederacy seemed to be in its death throes, and news of the war flooded across the telegraph network. According to reports, after sacking and burning Atlanta and leaving a swath of destruction across Georgia, Union General William Tecumseh Sherman and his army were now marching through the Carolinas. Then on April 3 news flashed across the telegraph that General Ulysses S. Grant's forces had captured Richmond, the Confederate capital, though Confederate president Jefferson Davis had fled south. The following day the news was of President Abraham Lincoln's visit to Richmond, where Lincoln had apparently sat for several minutes at Jefferson Davis's desk and savored the capture of the city.

Then on April 9, 1865, came even better news. Confederate General Robert E. Lee surrendered himself and his army to General Grant at Appomattox, Virginia. For all intents and purposes this marked the end of the Civil War, and the remaining pockets of Confederate resistance soon capitulated and surrendered to the Union.

What should have been a time of joy for those in the North quickly turned to despair on April 15, 1865, as the shocking news was carried across the nation by telegraph that President Abraham Lincoln had been assassinated the night before while attending a show at Ford's Theater in Washington, D.C. Tom felt a chill run down his spine when he heard the news chattering off the telegraph key in the office in Cincinnati.

By now Tom had a steady, well-paying job as a telegraph operator, but deep down inside this was not what he really wanted to do. As he had on so many jobs before, he refused to take his work seriously and instead used it as a backdrop for all kinds of experiments. And as had happened at his previous jobs, Tom's boss in Cincinnati soon grew tired of Tom's reckless attitude. Tom was fired and on his way again.

Over the next two years, Tom lost count of the jobs he held—and lost. He roamed the Midwest, taking a job here and a job there. He even headed south, thinking that he would take a job as a telegraph operator in Brazil. But when he reached New Orleans, the city was engulfed in race riots, and the U.S. government had commandeered all oceangoing ships to use to bring in federal troops to quell the riots. Among the vessels commandeered was the ship Tom had booked passage to Brazil on. His plans thwarted, Tom slowly made his way north again, often hungry and ill-clothed for the cold winter weather he encountered along the way.

By November 1867, Tom was back in Port Huron, jobless and without any money. At home he found his family in dire straits. The war had taken an economic toll on them all, and his parents were forced to take in boarders so that they would have money for food. Relations between his mother and his older brother Pitt were strained.

Often Tom found his mother sitting and staring into space, totally unaware of what was going on around her. That Christmas, however, Tom's mother was aware of a trick her younger son was playing on the guests who came to visit the house. Along the way in his travels, Tom has acquired a device called a Ruhmkorff induction coil that converted the electric current from a battery into high voltage. Tom surreptitiously rigged the coil up to the punch bowl so that anyone who dipped the ladle into the bowl received a hefty electric shock. Tom thought this was a hilarious practical joke, but his mother just shook her head. "I had such high hopes for you, boy," she lamented. "What went wrong?"

Tom did not have an answer for her.

Chapter 6

An Inventor—Finally

Two weeks after Christmas, Tom stood in front of the manager of the Western Union office in Boston, Massachusetts. For once in his life he felt self-conscious about the way he looked. He had on his usual outfit: a pair of jeans that were a couple of inches too short; a straw hat, even though it was the middle of winter; and a flannel shirt, several sizes too big for him, that draped over his five-foot-nine-inch, 135-pound body. He chewed on a wad of tobacco to cover his nervousness.

"So, do you want a job here?" the office manager asked.

Tom nodded. "Yes, sir. I can do thirty words a minute and write smaller than most people I know. I particularly like the press wires, because I read a lot and can often guess at what the missing words are."

"Umm," the manager replied, "come back tonight, and we'll see just what you're made of."

Tom walked out of the Western Union office elated. He knew that when given a chance he would always rise to the occasion, and so he did in this instance. Later that evening he was offered the coveted job of Number One Receiver on the press wire from New York City. The job involved decoding and writing down the news for the local newspapers as it was sent over the telegraph wire from New York.

It was the start Tom wanted, but he also had other ideas. He planned to set up his own workshop in Boston within a year and be done with the job of telegraph operator forever. His heart was set on becoming an inventor.

By all accounts Tom had come to the right place. Boston was the hub of research into the practical applications of electricity in the United States. Thomas Hall produced miniature electric trains, while Charles Williams Jr. ran a telegraphic and fine-instrument store. Not only that, Charles encouraged many young telegraph operators to experiment for themselves, providing cheap workshop space for several of them.

Tom found a cheap boardinghouse in which to live and set about making his dream come true. He realized that he needed a more methodical approach to developing his ideas, and so he started a habit that he would continue throughout the rest of his life. He bought a notebook and began to record all of his invention ideas and the experiments he carried out. When he hit the "big one," he would have a record and a timeline of its development that would enable him to obtain a patent for the device. A patent is a document that gives exclusive legal claim to an inventor for a particular invention he or she has invented, thus barring anyone else from reproducing a particular device without the patent holder's permission.

Tom did have an idea in mind to develop and to hopefully one day patent. It was an idea that he had been working on intermittently for over a year. He called it a duplex—a telegraphing machine that could transmit a message in both directions at the same time. At the time a telegraph wire could be used to send a message in only one direction. As a result, not enough wires were available to send all the messages needing to be sent, and so the messages would quickly back up awaiting transmission.

Other men in the telegraph business were working on the same problem, and Tom came up with one idea after another to try to solve it. Eventually he came up with a duplex that seemed to work, at least over the wires in the lab. But as was often the case, outside the lab, using telegraph wires exposed to the elements, the duplex did not behave as it was supposed to. As usual the situation frustrated Tom, but it also brought him some helpful exposure.

The *Telegrapher,* a scientific magazine founded by Frank L. Pope, one of the country's leading experts in telegraphy, was dedicated to reporting on advances in the fast-growing telegraph industry. When the magazine's editor heard of Tom's experiments in duplexing, the April 1868 issue of the magazine carried a long article about him. The magazine brought Tom to the attention of several men in

Boston interested in investing money in his enterprise. Tom was gratified.

The Civil War had spurred the growth of the telegraph as a means of communication throughout the country. Now that the war was over, the use of telegraphic technology was rapidly expanding. Businesses and even private homes were having telegraph lines installed to replace the messengers they relied on to deliver their communications. Aware of this growth and not wanting to be left out of it, Tom, while tinkering with his duplex, set his attention on another device—the gold ticker.

In 1863 the Gold Exchange had been established in New York City. Since the price of gold determined the price of other commodities, it was important for brokers and commodities dealers to know the price of gold hour by hour. This communication with the dealers and brokers had been carried out by an army of messenger boys who ran all over New York City carrying news of the latest price of gold. This was an unruly endeavor, and also noisy when the boys would burst into the Gold Exchange to check on the latest price.

In an attempt to keep the boys out of and the noise down in the Gold Exchange, a ticker device had been invented. The original ticker recorded the minute-by-minute price of gold on the exchange floor and sent the information to a display located in a window, where the messenger boys could check the gold price without having to enter the exchange floor. The ticker had become even more useful in 1866, when Frank L. Pope developed a device for capturing the information coming over the wire and printing it out in roman characters on a strip of paper. With the invention of this device, telegraph lines were run to offices all over New York City, where receiving devices were set up so that the price of gold could constantly and automatically be fed to the offices.

Tom partnered with two other telegraph operators, Bob Roberts and Frank Hanaford. Together the three men decided that they wanted to have a hand in seeing a gold ticker system installed in offices in Boston. Tom traveled to New York to meet Frank Pope and learn firsthand from him how the ticker operated. Frank was seven years older than Tom, and his knowledge of telegraphic technology was impressive. Tom learned much from him and returned to Boston with a transmitter and several tickers to start the new enterprise.

The first sale Tom and his partners made was to the banking firm of Kidder & Peabody. Other sales soon followed, and Tom and his partners were soon spending their days scurrying over roofs as they installed private telegraph lines and gold tickers to offices around Boston.

While Tom installed private telegraph lines and gold tickers by day, at night he would show up for his regular shift at the Western Union office. This soon changed as a result of the exposure the article in the *Telegrapher* magazine brought. Several of the men who had expressed interest in investing in his enterprise at the time of the article's publication offered Tom money, enough money to allow him to quit his regular job as a telegraph operator and devote himself to inventing. Tom wanted nothing more, and he quickly quit working for Western Union and set up a workshop and lab on Court Street in a building owned by Charles Williams Jr. Once the workshop and lab was up and running, Tom put a notice in the local telegraphic newspaper declaring that he, "Thomas A. Edison would hereafter devote his full time to bringing out his inventions."

Of course, now that he was a full-time inventor, Tom wondered what he should invent first. His answer came one day in Boston when he stopped to watch the members of the state legislature at work. The way that the legislators took votes seemed particularly cumbersome to Tom. The process could take hours, with each legislator standing and declaring whether he was a yes or a no vote. While this was going on, both sides were arguing back and forth, hoping to sway those legislators who had not yet voted. Tom was sure that an instant-voting machine was the answer to the apparent mayhem on the floor of the legislature. How much simpler was a device where each member pushed a yes or no button at the same time and the results were tallied within seconds.

Tom set to work on his instant-voting machine, using the same principle used in chemically recorded telegraphs. Each legislator's name was entered in metal type in a register, once in the yes column and once in the no column. When a vote was taken, the legislator would then flick either the yes or no switch, which in turn sent an electrical charge to the metal type bearing his name in the yes or no column. The clerk of the legislature would then lay a sheet of chemically treated paper over the metal register and then press it down with a metal roller. As the electrically charged type came in contact with the paper, it would burn off the chemicals at that spot, leaving the impression of the legislator's name in the yes or no column. The number of names in each column could then be quickly added up and the result of the vote known. When Tom was satisfied that the voting machine was ready, he applied for a patent for the device. The patent for his voting machine was issued on June 1, 1869.

Now that his patent had been granted, Tom rushed to show the voting machine to members of the Massachusetts legislature and explain to them how the machine would simplify their voting process. No one could have been more shocked than Tom when the first legislator he spoke to laughed in his face.

"I have no doubt your machine works," the man said, "but it's the last thing we want! Can you imagine if the votes were instant? How would we have the chance to change people's minds, to offer them deals if the vote wasn't going our way. No, son, some of our most important political work gets done between the time the vote starts and the time it finishes. Imagine—no time to filibuster!" The legislator then laughed some more.

Tom gulped and walked away. It was a sobering moment, but instantly he saw his error. He was the one who had thought that the voting machine would be a great idea. He had not asked those it was intended for whether or not they would use the device. As he walked back to the boardinghouse where he was living, Tom vowed that he would never again follow his whims; he would invent only those things that the public wanted and asked for. His inventions had to be practical—and make money.

In the wake of his failure to sell the legislature his voting machine, Tom turned his attention back to trying to improve the performance of his duplex. He also applied himself to improving on the gold ticker technology. In particular he focused on the need for a printer that could print all the letters of the alphabet and not just those letters and numbers needed to indicate the minute-by-minute price of gold. A printer that could print all the letters of the alphabet would make the telegraph a much more useful and appealing communications medium in homes, where an incoming message over the wire could automatically be printed out in readable type on paper. Such a device, Tom told himself, would surely speed the growth of telegraph lines into homes and offices, and he would be there to install the lines for them and sell them one of his printers.

Developing a printer of the kind he envisioned was a difficult challenge for Tom and took much longer than he had thought it would take. At the same time, his improved duplex failed again in out-door tests, and in the light of this failure and that of the voting machine, Tom's financial backers decided to withdraw their financial support of him.

With the help of one of his partners, Frank Hanaford, Tom tried to keep going with his invent-ing, but soon, not surprisingly, Tom and Frank were running short of money. They tried to look for more financial backers, but it seemed that no one in Boston was willing to lend them money. But they needed money—and quickly—to keep developing the duplex and the printer, not to mention to maintain their existing gold ticker business. Tom decided that he should set out for New York City in the hope that Frank Pope would understand what they were trying to do and give them the needed capital to keep going.

Tom caught a steamer down the coast from Boston to New York. But with only two dollars in his pocket, he found himself in a bind when he arrived in New York. He did not want to appear desperate to Frank Pope, yet he had nowhere to stay and little money to spend on food. Soon he came up with a solution to his problem, or so he thought. He had traveled around so much as a telegraph operator that he was sure he would find a telegrapher somewhere in New York whom he knew. Surely, an old acquaintance would lend him a few dollars and point the way to a cheap boardinghouse.

It took less than a day for this plan to fall apart. Tom did find one person he knew at the Western Union office, but the man appeared to be as broke as Tom and had no cheap lodgings to recommend. So Tom was forced to spend the rest of the day and the entire night wandering around New York City. He wasn't too worried yet, but he was hungry.

In the morning Tom noticed a man in a shop entrance trying to sell small bags of tea. The man was so eager to sell his wares that he even gave a sample to one customer to take home. Even though

Tom had no home to take a teabag back to, he lined up and asked the vendor for a sample. Tom then went to the nearest coffee shop and asked if he could exchange his bag of tea for a cup of coffee, which was much cheaper than tea, and something to eat. The waitress agreed and provided Tom with a steaming hot cup of coffee and an apple dumpling in exchange for the tea. Tom had to admit that it was the most delicious apple dumpling he had ever eaten.

Buoyed by having hot coffee and apple dumpling in his stomach, Tom decided on a new plan. He would go straight to visit Frank Pope, explain his situation to him, and ask for help. With that settled, Tom walked determinedly toward the Gold Indicator Company headquarters, where Frank worked.

Tom was shown to Frank's office, and the two men greeted each other warmly. Frank listened as Tom told his tale of woe. While he was not eager to lend Tom and Frank Hanaford the money they sought for their Boston venture, he was willing to employ Tom as a temporary mechanic. When he realized that Tom did not have a place to stay, he offered him a cot in the company's battery room located in the basement of the Mills Building on Broad Street. With no alternative, Tom accepted the offer and moved his few belongings into the battery room and reported for work at the Gold Indicator Company. His job mainly involved keeping the various machines in good working order and repairing them when they broke down.

In many ways it was a carefree time in Tom's life. Tom could eat, breathe, and sleep machines, except for one problem: he was supposed to be raising money to take back to Boston. And the news he was receiving from Frank Hanaford was alarming. The batteries that powered the gold ticker system were not lasting well, the printers were regularly breaking down, and many of the lines were falling. Tom became desperate wondering what he should do. There was no point in going back to Boston without money, and he was not having much luck gathering any in New York. He wrote back to Frank.

It would appear from what has happened already that the gray-eyed spectre of destiny has been our guardian angel for no matter what I may do I reap nothing but trouble and blues. Please do all you can till I get the Printers ready, and put them on the line, you ought to know me well enough to know that I am neither a dead beat or a selfish person and that I always do as I agree without some…ill luck prevents it. However, I'll never give up for I may have a streak of luck before I die.

A few days after penning these words to Frank, Tom experienced one such streak of luck. When a spring broke on one of the company's main transmitting machines, causing the device to jam, the Gold Indicator Company was thrown into turmoil. The receiving devices at the various brokers' offices ran wild with incorrect information. Soon the building was filled with the sound of men and boys yelling and rushing to see what had gone wrong. Tom raced to the broken machine and quickly discovered what the problem was. Just then, Samuel Laws, owner of the Gold Indicator Company and the original inventor of the gold ticker, raced into the room yelling, "Fix it! Fix It!"

Tom was already on the job, and two hours later he had repaired the machine and had it running again. However, that was not the end of the problem. Each of the erratically behaving receivers in the various brokers' offices had to be reset by hand, a time-consuming task.

Seeing the nature of the problem, Tom approached Mr. Laws. He explained that he could construct a device that would stop all the receivers in unison and so stop them from running wild as they had done when the main transmitting machine had broken. Mr. Laws knew right away that such a device could save him both time and money. He questioned Tom about his ability to construct such a machine. When he had satisfied himself that Tom had the ability, he told him that if he was able to build a device that worked and caused the receivers to stop in unison, he would promote him to the position of supervisor, with a salary of $225 a month.

Tom accepted the offer and set to work. Since he saw no point in returning to Boston, he wrote to Frank Hanaford and explained that he would keep working on the Boston problems from New York and save as much money as he could to send back to Frank. Tom's plans were interrupted, however, when Samuel Laws unexpectedly sold the Gold Indicator

Company to his competitor, the Gold and Stock Company, and Tom was once again out of a job.

Frank Pope was also out of a job, and he soon came up with a solution. He, his business partner and lifelong friend, James Ashley, and Tom, would join forces and form a company to compete with the Gold and Stock Company. Tom jumped at the opportunity, and the Financial and Commercial Telegraph Company was formed.

From sleeping in the battery room at the Gold Indicator Company, Tom went to stay at Frank Pope's parents' luxurious home in Elizabeth, New Jersey, and the new company rented a workshop nearby. Everyone set to work. James marketed the new company's products and services while Frank handled the financial side of things. And Tom did what he loved to do—invent. He had developed new ideas for a printing device, and he was rising early and not returning home until after midnight.

During the long winter of 1869 Tom was often cold and exhausted, yet he tried to stay optimistic as he looked toward the future. He confided to Frank Hanaford in a letter, "Keep your courage up and it will come out all right. Think I can get you a red hot situation here where you can make some stamps. My hair is...near white. Man told me yesterday I was a walking churchyard."

Within a month the situation had changed for Tom. Frank Pope had brokered a deal with Marshall Lefferts, president of the Gold and Stock Company. Although the company Tom and his partners had started was tiny, Tom had applied for a number of patents that Lefferts desperately wanted to get his hands on. The deal Frank had brokered called for their small company to sell its patents to the Gold and Stock Company for the sum of fifteen thousand dollars in installments.

Tom was completely shocked when, in New York, Lefferts wrote him a check for fifteen hundred dollars. He stared at the check for a long time, unable to comprehend that he was holding so much money. Finally he tucked the check into his pocket and walked off down the street. He supposed he should take the check to a bank, but Tom had never had a bank account before and was unsure of how to open one. He wandered down Broadway and walked into the nearest bank. The bank was a big and imposing building. Tom stepped nervously up to the counter, aware of how shabby he looked in his work clothes.

"I'd like to start an account here," he said to the teller, handing over his check.

The bank teller looked at the check closely, and then turned it over. "It's no good without your endorsement," he said.

Tom looked around. He felt like everyone was looking at him. He did not know what the teller meant, and he was too embarrassed to ask. What did he mean the check was no good? Maybe he meant that the check was a hoax. Had Marshall Lefferts been playing a practical joke on him when he gave Tom that much money? Tom didn't know. What he did know was that he did not belong in a bank. He grabbed his check and fled the building.

Chapter 7

Doing Business

Tom walked the streets of Manhattan for an hour before he calmed down enough to return to Marshall Leffert's office to unravel the situation. He explained to Leffert's secretary that the bank had rejected the check.

The secretary laughed. "Don't tell me you've never cashed a check before," she said.

"No," Tom admitted. "I've always been paid in cash, and I liked it a lot better that way."

"Don't you know that you have to sign the back of a check before the bank will give you the money?"

Again, Tom had to admit to the secretary that this was a new concept to him.

The secretary smiled, grabbed her hat and coat, and walked Tom to the bank. She stayed with him while he endorsed the check and received fifteen hundred dollars in cash. It was such a large amount of money that the bills would not fit in his pockets, so Tom padded his clothes with them. He felt like a scarecrow.

That night Tom should have been out celebrating, but he was too terrified to leave the money in his room. Instead he sat up most of the night staring at the pile of bills. The next morning when he emerged from his room, he looked exhausted. A friend suggested that Tom deposit the money into a savings account and let the bank worry about taking care of it. This was another new concept to Tom, but he gladly took the money to a bank, opened an account, and exchanged the money for a savings passbook.

Now Tom had to decide what to do next and, more particularly, what invention he should concentrate on. He could not imagine spending his money on anything except materials to keep him inventing and experimenting. Soon Tom learned that Lefferts wanted to make a deal with him. Lefferts wanted Tom to go into business with an associate of his, William Unger. The new firm would then focus on producing a new and improved stock ticker. The Gold and Stock Company was in fierce competition with the Western Union Company for control of transmitting financial information. However, the tickers, or printers, that Western Union was using were troublesome, and Lefferts realized that if he had a better ticker, he would have a decided advantage over his rival in the field of transmitting financial information. And who better to develop this new ticker than Thomas Edison, whose reputation as an innovator in the field of telegraphic equipment was growing rapidly.

According to Tom's agreement with Lefferts, when Tom had produced the prototype for the new ticker, the Gold and Stock Company would place a substantial order for the new ticker with the firm of Edison and Unger. Such an order would be very lucrative for Tom. It sounded like a good plan to Tom, especially since it left him free to pursue other opportunities.

The firm of Edison and Unger rented workshop space in Newark, New Jersey, and Tom set to work on developing an improved stock ticker. By October 1870 he had perfected the device. It was time to show it to Lefferts. Tom put on a suit, propped a top hat on his head, and set out for New York.

At the Gold and Stock Company Lefferts was impressed with the new ticker, especially when Tom explained how it overcame a deficiency of earlier tickers that would cause them to sometimes run erratically, creating problems down the line and across the whole ticker network.

"And how much would you want for the patent to the ticker, Tom?" Lefferts asked.

Tom secretly hoped to get five thousand dollars for the patent to his new ticker, but he was willing to settle for three thousand dollars. To Tom these were astronomical sums of money, and he could not muster the nerve to say out loud the amount he wanted. Instead he replied, "Well, suppose you make me an offer."

Marshall Lefferts nodded. "All right," he said. "How does forty thousand dollars strike you?"

Tom was speechless and for a moment thought he might faint. Forty thousand dollars—that was a fortune! Finally he managed to regain his composure. "I think that's fair," he stammered as he reached out to shake Leffert's hand and seal the deal.

With forty thousand dollars in the bank, Tom had enough money to set up a much larger workshop and lab in Newark. In the winter of 1870 the firm of Edison and Unger settled on an old four-story brick building on Ward Street as the location for its expanded premises. Newark was a thriving city, a financial center for New Jersey, with a good labor pool and other resources to draw from. Like Edison and Unger, a number of other industries had located their operations there. As well, Newark was also only nine miles from New York City, one of the main markets for Tom's inventions. Tom ordered equipment and materials for the new location and began hiring more employees to man the much larger facility.

Tom's plan for the larger Edison and Unger was twofold. Half the time Tom would have his men work on making telegraphic machines such as tickers, transmitters, perforators, ink recorders, and printers. By now he was fortunate enough to have an order for twelve hundred of the new, improved tickers, for which Western Union, who had taken over the Gold and Stock Company, was willing to pay $125 apiece. The rest of the time Tom planned to have his workers build experimental devices or try to improve and perfect existing inventions.

Running the much larger workshop at Edison and Unger kept Tom very busy. He wished he had the time to go back home to Port Huron and visit his parents and tell them about his change in fortune. But alas, he had no time to spare. Instead he sent them gifts, money, and letters. One letter read:

Dear Father and Mother,

I sent you another express package Saturday, enclosed you will find the receipt for the same.

I C Edison [a cousin] writes me that mother is not very well and that you have to work very hard. I guess you had better take it easy after this. Don't do any hard work and get mother anything she desires. You can draw on me for the money. Write me and say how much money you will need till June and I will send the amount on the first of that month. Give love to all folks. And write me the town news...

Your affec. Son
Thomas A.

Tom continued to worry about his elderly parents, but he could do little apart from sending them gifts and money. He was far too busy hiring workers and setting up equipment. Soon he had assembled a brilliant team of workers who streamlined the process of inventing. Tom liked to think of the ideas and sketch them out on paper. But his hand-eye coordination was not the best, and his sketches were fairly rudimentary, more like the drawings of a student than of a famous inventor. It then fell to Charles Batchelor, an Englishman two years older than Tom and a trained draftsman, to take Tom's sketches and turn them into meticulous blueprints and then develop a detailed plan for executing the creation of the new invention. With the technical drawings in hand, John Kruesi, a twenty-nine-year-old Swiss machinist who had worked for the Singer Sewing Machine Company before joining Tom, began to build a working model of the device. In the building process, John drew on the skills and talents of many of the other men working for the company.

With Charles and John to help him steer the design and manufacturing process, things went along smoothly for Tom, except in one area. Tom had no system at all for handling the new venture's finances. He knew little about money and did not want to learn. The whole matter of money was a bother to him and a distraction from his work. At first Marshall Lefferts, whose Gold and Stock Company was now part of Western Union, loaned Tom one of his company's bookkeepers to help out, since Tom was doing so much work for Western Union.

Tom was fine with the new bookkeeping arrangement, and at one stage the bookkeeper announced that the company had a surplus of seventy-five hundred dollars. Tom was delighted and immediately threw a big party and ordered more equipment. However, a number of days later, debtors came knocking at the door looking for payment, and Tom then realized that he had not handed over the paperwork for several large orders for equipment. By the time all the uncalculated debts were added in, the company had gone from having a surplus of seventy-five hundred dollars to being three thousand dollars in debt.

The bookkeeper quit, and Tom, who blamed the bookkeeper for the financial mess, refused to have another one. Instead, he hammered two hooks into the wall above his desk. One hook was for the money he owed people, and the other was for money that had been paid to him. Tom "filed" all his bills on the money-owed hook, but having done so, he never looked at a bill again. Rather he waited for a letter threatening legal action or cutting off some service before he paid the bill. The way Tom figured it, the longer he could stretch paying someone, the more money he had to build things. In fact, Tom was soon involved in so many business deals that he could not keep them all straight in his head.

Deep down, Tom did not care how much debt he incurred or how many deals he signed, as long as the money kept coming in so that he could keep inventing. He was soon involved in five contracts, all with deadlines and stiff penalties for failing to meet those deadlines.

Still, one way or another, the process of inventing and improving continued. More often than not Tom and his crew would have to work through the night to finish things by the promised contract deadlines. The standard workweek for Tom's employees was ten hours a day, six days a week, but many of the men routinely worked sixteen to eighteen hours a day, taking their weekly total number of hours worked to around one hundred. Tom drove himself even harder. He lived on strong coffee, pie, cigars, and chewing tobacco and slept an average of four hours a night, often on a workbench in the workshop, using the crook of his elbow as a pillow.

Early in April 1871, two months after his twenty-fourth birthday, Tom received a telegram bearing bad news. His sixty-one-year-old mother had died. Feeling guilty that he had not taken the time to visit his parents sooner, he rushed home to Port Huron for the funeral. As he stood beside his mother's grave, Tom wished that his mother could have visited Newark and seen how successful her son had become. He recalled how she had been the only one who had believed that as a child he was not addled, and how she had let him explore his own interests when she taught him at home. And now she was gone.

When he returned to Newark, Tom threw himself back into his work. He soon received an order for thirty thousand dollars' worth of his new and improved stock tickers, or the Edison stock printer, as the device was now called. Tom and his men set to work updating and improving the stock ticker to fulfill the order, but they ran into a problem. The new tickers would not work right. The design had some kind of bug in it that prevented the tickers from doing all that they were designed to do.

The delivery date for the tickers was approaching, and Tom did not want to lose the order. But try as he may, he could not seem to work out the bug and get the ticker working right. Finally, in desperation, Tom called his most trusted group of associates together in a room on the fourth floor. After they had all entered the room, he locked the door behind them.

"Men," Tom announced, "I've locked the door, and we are all going to stay locked in here until we've figured out why this device doesn't work right. So let's get busy."

The surprised men rolled up their sleeves and began studying the problem.

One day passed, and the men still had not solved the problem. They had little food to eat and even less sleep as they tried one possible solution after another. Some of the wives of the men locked in the room came and banged on the door and pleaded with Tom to let their husbands out, but he refused. He even refused to unlock the door to receive the baskets of food the women had brought for the men to eat.

Hunger and lack of sleep seemed to spur the men on. Tom supposed that they feared he might let them starve to death. Nevertheless, the approach worked, and after two and a half days locked in the room, the men discovered what the problem was and worked out a solution. The new ticker worked flawlessly. Satisfied with the solution and that the contract delivery date for the tickers would be met, Tom unlocked the door, and his by-now bedraggled men headed home for a long overdue meal and some sleep.

Despite his focus on hard work, during this time Tom made the acquaintance of his future wife. Her name was Mary Stilwell, and she was a ticker-tape puncher in his factory. Tom loved to watch Mary work; she had beautiful grey eyes and long golden hair.

It was difficult for the relationship to progress beyond a daydream, since Tom was not used to talking to girls and had absolutely no idea how to make small talk. His world was a man's world of lathes and pulleys and levers. And being partly deaf did not help either.

Still, in October Tom gathered his courage and smiled at Mary, and she smiled back at him. "What do you think of me?" he asked.

Mary turned bright red. "Why, Mr. Edison, you frighten me," she stammered, "Well, what I mean is..."

Tom nodded. "Don't be in a hurry telling me. It doesn't matter much what you think unless you would like to marry me," he said, cutting Mary off.

Mary looked down at her work and nervously fidgeted with some ticker tape, and Tom walked away.

It was not a great start to a romance, but what Tom lacked in tact he made up for in tenaciousness. He asked Mary to accompany him to the theater, and she did, along with her older sister Alice, who acted as their chaperone. Soon the three of them were regularly going to the theater and to music halls.

By the beginning of December Tom decided that he wanted Mary to be his wife. Mary's background was similar to his. Her father was a woodcutter who had struggled to make a living for his wife and a host of children and stepchildren. Tom talked to Mr. Stilwell about marrying his daughter. Mr. Stilwell responded by asking Tom to wait a year, because Mary was just sixteen and the two of them had known each other for less than a year. But Tom was not accustomed to waiting for anything, and so he went ahead and planned the wedding for Christmas Day, 1871.

The wedding was a small affair, and after the ceremony Tom returned to his workshop. He had one more idea he wanted to try out before he went off on their honeymoon to Niagara Falls the next day. He did not arrive home until midnight, where he found Mary anxiously pacing the floor of their newly rented house as she waited for him.

The next day Mary was so distraught about leaving her family behind and going away with Tom that he bought another ticket, and Mary's sister Alice accompanied them on their honeymoon.

When they got back to Newark, Tom and Mary began their married life together. Tom resumed his eighteen-hour days working at the workshop and continued with his habit of sleeping there at night. Alice moved into the house to keep her sister company.

It was not long before Tom realized the folly of marrying someone so young. Mary had no idea how to handle the family finances. Tom gave her a generous allowance with which to run the house, but she spent much of the money on candies, oysters, music-hall visits with her sister, and trips into New York City to buy the latest fashions. It was not long before the butcher and the baker were calling at the house, demanding payment of their bills.

Within a month of Tom's getting married, his father came to visit him in Newark and inspect his new daughter-in-law. Samuel Edison also brought a request to Tom from his brother Pitt. It seemed that Pitt had invested the little money he had in a horse-car line in Port Huron. But the horsecar business was in deep financial trouble, and Pitt was close to losing all his money. He wanted Tom to loan him $3,100 to save him from going bankrupt.

This was a large sum of money, but Tom handed a check for the amount over to his father to deliver to Pitt. Tom was confident that even if his brother could not repay the money, his inventions would generate enough money to easily cover the debt. Had Tom known what lay ahead, he might have been a little more cautious.

Chapter 8

A Generous Offer

Tom turned to William Unger. "You want to what?" he asked incredulously.

"I want to dissolve our partnership. We've finished our contract with the Gold and Stock Company, the last of the twelve hundred tickers has been delivered, and I've had enough."

"Enough?" Tom asked. "Why, we're only getting started. We made a profit, didn't we?"

William grimaced. "If you mean all our debts are paid, you're right, but we should have made a lot more. So much of the money went to pay the men wages when they were working on your experiments. And we don't have any profit to show for those experiments."

Tom sighed. He was so tired of unscientific people running his affairs. "Of course, there isn't an instant profit. That's why it's an experiment."

"Whatever you call it, I want out," William said flatly. "The way I figure it, if we sell the workshop and the machines, we can divide the proceeds. According to my calculations, your share would be $3,649."

Tom spluttered. His business partner was serious. He really did want to sell everything. "Let me think about it for a day or two," Tom said, unwilling to trust himself to go on with the conversation.

For the next several days Tom thought of little else but the future of Edison and Unger. He could not bear the thought of selling the workshop and machines. Where would he invent? And what would happen to the wonderful team of workers he had built up? No, he told himself, there had to be another solution. And there was.

Tom decided that he would buy out William's share of the business. He would give William $2,500 in cash and a promissory note for another $5,000 and assume the $60,045 of debt the company owed. To finance the buyout, Tom borrowed money from the Republic Trust Company.

By June 1872 the Edison and Unger Company was no more. Tom was now in business on his own, and for the next few months things moved at a feverish pace. Tom hired Joseph Murray to take over running the daytime operations of the workshop, while he took over the night shift. Tom and a small group of dedicated workers, including Charles Batchelor and John Kruesi, would work through the night improving on various aspects of telegraphy. By September Tom had applied for thirteen new patents. He was also working on a domestic telegraph system, imagining how useful it would be if people at home could telegraph the police or fire brigade in case of an emergency. The newly invented typewriter also caught Tom's attention.

The first practical typewriter had been invented by Christopher Latham Sholes, and the Remington Arms Company began producing and marketing the machine. The device had metal type attached to the end of bars, so that when a particular key was pushed, the bar would pop up, causing the metal type to strike an ink-impregnated ribbon placed in front of a rotary rubber cylinder around which a sheet of paper was wound. As the type forced the ribbon against the paper, it left the mark of the particular letter.

Tom had to admit it was an ingenious contraption, but the typewriter had some drawbacks, the biggest being the way the type bars often jammed if the keys were pushed too quickly one after the other. To fix this problem, Christopher Sholes had obtained a list of the most common letters used in English and rearranged the layout of his keyboard. Instead of the letters being laid out alphabetically, the keys were changed so that the most common pairs of letters were spread far apart on the keyboard. This arrangement forced the person typing to slow down as he or she searched for the various keys, and this slowing down caused fewer jams of the type bars. But as a person memorized the layout of the keyboard, he or she began to type faster, and the jamming problem became a recurring annoyance.

As Tom studied the typewriter, he decided that he could improve on its design, and he got to work. Instead of having type bars, Tom's device had an electric-powered wheel that rotated to the particular letter when its key was pushed. Once the letter was lined up, an electromagnetic pulse would cause it to strike the paper and leave an impression of the letter. The device was impressive when it was finished. Not only did it work much faster than Sholes's typewriter, it did not jam. The new machine had just one problem. The battery needed to power it was so large, and the power drain from it so great, that the new typewriter was impractical for everyday use and thus was not a commercially viable product. Still, Tom was proud of his achievement, not to mention the sheer enjoyment the project had brought him.

The fact that Tom had applied for and received so many new patents in his new venture did not tell the whole story. The truth was, he needed someone to dole out the money to him because he was spending it faster than he could make it. By early winter he had borrowed four hundred dollars from the Gold and Stock Company and had not yet been able to pay William the balance he had promised he would pay him. There was also the matter of the nine thousand dollars' worth of unpaid bills. Something had to be done to try and stabilize Tom's finances, especially since Mary was expecting a baby early the following year. Tom took a job with the Automatic Telegraph Company, working to improve the efficiency of the company's telegraphic equipment. It was not an ideal situation, but the job paid Tom a salary of two thousand dollars a year—money he desperately needed if he was to get out of debt.

On Christmas Day 1872, Tom and Mary Edison quietly passed their first wedding anniversary. Two months later, on February 18, 1873, Mary gave birth to a daughter, whom they named Marion. Two months after the birth of Marion, on April 23, 1873, Tom was standing on the aft deck of a steamer watching the Manhattan skyline recede from view. He was on his way to England!

The telegraph system in England was run by the post office and used equipment that would not work over a distance of more than forty miles. As a result, the post-office officials were very interested in Tom and his improved telegraph equipment, which could work over much greater distances. They were especially interested in employing his equipment on their lines to Scotland, Ireland, and France.

On the trip to England Tom was accompanied by an assistant, Jack Wright. On their arrival in London, the pair went to stay at a hotel in Covent Garden. The next day they made their way to the post office on Telegraph Road and set up their equipment to run a number of demonstrations. Once the equipment was set up in London, Jack headed for Liverpool to set up equipment there also.

When the telegraphic equipment was in place, Tom began his demonstration. But things did not go well. The batteries the British used to power their system were weak, and many of their wires were corroded, causing electricity to leak, further weakening the overall power of the system. An expensive one-hundred-cell battery, the most powerful battery in the world, was quickly purchased and attached to the system. Things worked much better then, and the post-office officials were impressed with the power of Tom's system. Tom was able to get his equipment transmitting and receiving in Morse code over one hundred words per minute between London and Liverpool.

The next thing that the post-office officials wanted to see firsthand was how well Tom's equipment worked over underwater cables, which were used to connect England to Ireland and France. To run this test, Tom was furnished with a large tank that contained coiled cable. Working with an underwater cable was new for Tom, since in the United States his equipment was used on wires hung from poles. Still, as he connected his equipment to either end of the cable, Tom expected it to work just as it did on land, that is, until he sent his first message— a 1/32-inch dot. Unfortunately, when it printed on the other end, the tiny dot stretched out for twenty-seven feet!

Tom was dumbfounded. He had no explanation for the anomaly. And no matter how many times he tried sending a message over the cable, he could not get it to work right. What could the problem be? Tom scratched his head in bewilderment. Of course it did not help that the British post-office officials were breathing down his neck, expecting him to come up with an immediate solution before they would invest in his system. But somehow Tom could not manage to get his head around the problem.

In the end Tom decided that the reason he could not think the problem through was his diet. Back home he normally existed on a diet of pie and coffee. But since arriving in England, he had been eating flounder and roast beef and drinking tea. "My imagination was getting into a coma," he observed, "[so]

I found a French pastry shop in High Holborn Street and filled up. My imagination got all right."

Despite stuffing himself daily on French pastries and coffee throughout the rest of his stay in England, Tom could not seem to get his head around the problem with the cable transmission. After six weeks in England, Tom decided that he needed a less-pressured environment in which to focus on the problem, and he announced that he was returning home to the United States.

Tom arrived home discouraged. Since he had not been able to solve the problem with the cable, he had not been able to close any lucrative deal with the post office in England to purchase his equip-ment. Tom would work on solving the cable prob-lem, but more than anything, he wanted to get back to inventing. As he walked into his workshop in Newark, the next thing he wanted to focus on was improving the duplex system.

Before long, Tom and his team had developed the diplex. While the duplex would allow two messages, one in either direction along a line at the same time, the diplex allowed two messages at a time to be sent down a wire in the same direction.

In January 1874, with work on the diplex com-plete, Tom focused on an even greater challenge— the quadruplex. While the diplex could send two messages at the same time down a telegraph wire, the quadruplex was designed to send two messages along a line in either direction at the same time.

Then in March, with work on the development of the quadruplex almost complete, Tom formed the Domestic Telegraph Company to market and install domestic telegraph lines into homes, allowing people to send emergency messages to the police and fire departments.

By July 1874, despite Tom's hard work on his inventions and various business ventures, money troubles once again raised their head. Tom was faced with the real possibility that he would have to go bankrupt. As usual, though, he was not about to give up without a fight, and eventually he was able to obtain a loan from the Automatic Telegraph Company to stave off bankruptcy.

Later that year Tom's nephew Charles, his brother Pitt's son, came from Port Huron to work for him. Charley was barely a teenager, but Tom saw in the boy a lot of himself at the same age. He did his best to encourage his nephew's inquisitive ways and inventive spirit.

Around the time Charley came to work for his uncle, Tom began trying to sell the now-completed quadruplex. Western Union was already using his diplex system, and the company was eager to see the quadruplex at work. Tom went to company headquarters in Manhattan and demonstrated just what the quadruplex could do. William Orton, the president of Western Union, immediately saw the value of the device. The quadruplex would lead to better utilization of the company's telegraph lines by exponentially increasing the volume of messages that could be carried over them. It would also lead to the company's having to string fewer new lines in the coming years, bringing big savings in what was a large yearly capital expenditure for Western Union.

Tom was aware of these advantages as he set about negotiating a suitable price with Orton for the quadruplex. He pointed out that the quadruplex would immediately create the equivalent of fifty thousand miles of additional telegraph lines, helping Western Union protect its monopoly on the sending and receiving of telegraphs. Tom proposed that Western Union pay him one twentieth of the cost of maintaining fifty thousand miles of line for seventeen years, the length of his patent on the quadruplex. Tom supposed this amount to be about $450,000. William Orton listened attentively to Tom's proposal before informing him that he had no intention of paying Tom that much money for the quadruplex.

Over the next several days, the two men haggled over the cost of the quadruplex. Finally, several days before Christmas, Orton made Tom his final offer. Western Union was prepared to pay him twenty thousand dollars up front and then ten thousand dollars a year for the next ten years for the quadruplex. Orton was about to leave for Chicago for Christmas and New Year and informed Tom that he would give him that time to think over the deal.

Tom left the Western Union office feeling frustrated and unhappy with the company's offer. As far as he was concerned, the quadruplex was worth a lot more than what he was being offered for it. That was when Tom received word that Jay Gould wanted to meet with him to talk about the quadruplex. Gould was one of the richest men in America, and he was secretly plotting to strike at Western Union's telegraphic transmission monopoly in the

United States. He had been quietly buying up small telegraph companies across the country and had formed them into the Atlantic and Pacific Telegraph Company. Now he was interested in deploying the quadruplex, which would give the new company a decided edge over its rival in the volume of messages it could transmit.

On January 4, 1875, Tom had a skip in his step as he approached Gould's mansion on Fifth Avenue. He reminded himself that a man as rich as Jay Gould could afford to make him a handsome offer for his device, and Tom was determined not to sell himself short, as William Orton wanted him to do.

Gould's home was even more magnificent than Tom could have imagined. Priceless works of art lined the wood-paneled walls, and deep-piled Persian carpets covered the floors. And although he had bathed and put on his best suit before setting out for the meeting, Tom felt shabby in such luxurious surroundings.

Soon Jay Gould entered the living room and shook Tom's hand, and the two men fell into conversation. Gould wanted the rights to Tom's quadruplex, and in exchange he offered Tom the position of "electrician," basically the manager of technical affairs, for the Atlantic and Pacific Telegraph Company, along with seventy-five thousand dollars in company stock and twenty-five thousand dollars in cash.

Tom was astonished by the generous offer, but he tried to look concerned. "That's a bit small," he told Gould, shaking his head.

"How about thirty thousand in cash then?" Gould responded, upping the cash amount by five thousand dollars.

"All right," Tom agreed. "I think I can live with that."

"Would you like the money now or later?" Gould asked.

"I'll take some of it now," Tom informed him.

Gould waved his arm. "Then follow me," he said.

The two of them made their way downstairs to Gould's office, where a muscle-bound bodyguard sat behind a walnut desk. Gould quickly drew up an agreement giving him the rights to the quadruplex, and Tom signed it. The agreement signed, the bodyguard opened the vault and handed Tom ten thousand dollars in cash.

Tom left Jay Gould's mansion elated. Now he could pay the milkman, the grocer, and the doctor, who had all been hounding him for the money he owed them. But more important, Tom could get on with the big plans he had for a new invention factory like nothing the world had ever seen before!

Chapter 9

The Wizard of Menlo Park

Menlo Park. I like that name. And it's in the country, you say, twelve miles from Newark?" Tom said to his young friend William Carman as he studied a map in late 1875.

"Yes, sir, twelve miles in the country." William replied. "One of the houses, a large two-story place, is for sale, and my family has eight acres of gently rolling pastureland nearby that they are also willing to sell."

"Ummm," Tom mused. "It would certainly be great to be out in the country—no more neighbors complaining about the noise at night, no more high rents. And how far is it to the nearest railroad?"

"Runs right through Menlo Park on the way to Jersey City," William replied. "Has its own telegraph booth, and the Lincoln Highway runs through the place."

The location sounded promising, and when Tom and William took the train out to see the place, Tom knew that he had found the perfect spot for his new invention laboratory. The house was spacious, just what he and Mary needed now that Mary was expecting their second child. And the plot of land was perfect, located on a rise near the railroad.

On December 29, 1875, Tom signed an agreement to purchase the house and the parcel of land at Menlo Park. He also convinced Charles Batchelor and John Kruesi to buy houses neighboring the property. Twelve days later, on January 10, 1876, Mary Edison gave birth to a son in Newark, whom they named Thomas Alva Edison Jr.

Now that he had purchased land in Menlo Park, Tom invited his father to supervise the building of a laboratory on the site. Tom's nephew Charley also came to assist with the building. Work on the structure began in January 1876, and soon the one-hundred-foot-long, two-storied building made of rough-hewn hemlock was taking shape. The laboratory looked like an enormous barn and was situated only three hundred yards from the railroad track. Tom had all sorts of machinery freighted to Menlo Park by rail, and the men who lugged it up to the new building appreciated the lab's location close to the railroad.

The new structure was completed in March 1876. When finished it was lined from floor to ceiling with shelves, with twenty-five hundred bottles of chemicals arranged on them. Various workstations were set up with batteries and telegraphic equipment ready to be used in experiments.

With the new laboratory complete, Tom moved his base of operation from Newark to Menlo Park, and he, Mary, Marion, and new baby Thomas moved into their new home. Marion, whom Tom called "Dot," and Thomas, who was soon nicknamed "Dash," after the Morse code symbols, thrived in the countryside.

While Tom had been searching for the right piece of land on which to build his new invention factory, he had kept busy conducting experiments on another device—the electric pen and autographic printing. Tom and Charles had decided that there was an opening in the market for a process that would allow people, and particularly businesses, to reproduce multiple copies of an original document. To aid this process, Tom devised the electric pen. The device functioned somewhat as a pen, but instead of having a nib, this pen had a needle. An electromagnetic motor connected to a galvanic battery powered the device. In turn the motor spun a small flywheel that caused the needle of the pen to reciprocate, or go up and down. The pen operator would then write on a sheet of specially treated wax paper. As he wrote, the needle would make evenly spaced small perforations through the paper, creating a written document where the letters were formed not by ink on the page but by tiny holes that formed outlines of the letters.

The waxed page with the holes then became a stencil for the autographic printing process. When a stencil had been punched with the electric pen, a felt roller was used to apply printer's ink to the page. The ink pooled in the tiny holes in the stencil, which was then placed over a clean sheet of paper. Another roller was pressed over the stencil, forcing some of the ink out of the holes and onto the clean page, creating an exact copy of the stencil. A number of exact copies could be made from the stencil before it had to be re-inked.

Satisfied with the new device and the autographic printing process, Tom applied for a patent for it on March 13, 1876, just as he was moving into his new house and laboratory in Menlo Park. The patent was soon granted, and production and marketing of the electric pen began. The electric pen sold for thirty-five dollars, complete with ink, rollers, a frame to hold the pages in place while copies were being made, and an instruction manual. In fact, the electric pen was the first electric appliance to be produced and marketed in the United States. Soon Tom was selling electric pens to people all over the country. An advertising flyer hailed the electric pen as able to duplicate "Letters, Circulars, Price Lists, Market Quotations, Circular Letters, Pamphlets, Catalogues, Lawyer's Briefs, Legal Documents, Manifests, Labels, Letter and Billheads, Maps, Architectural and Mechanical Outline Drawings, Music, Cypher, Codes, Press Reports, Financial Exhibits, Ruled Forms and Artistic Drawing."

With development of the electric pen behind him, and now ensconced in his new lab and workshop at Menlo Park, Tom had a long list of other things he wished to invent and experiment with. These included electric scissors, a revolving display cabinet, a dental drill, an artificial perfumed rose, a refillable cigar, and an electric sewing machine. But before Tom had time to fully settle into his new life at Menlo Park, he learned about an incredible experiment conducted by a Scottish immigrant in Boston. The man, Alexander Graham Bell, had set up a workshop in Charles Williams's building in Boston, the same building in which Tom had established his small lab nine years before.

Bell and his young assistant, Thomas Watson, had been working on a device they called the telephone, or "far speaker," which could transmit a spoken voice over a wire. After many failed attempts, Bell and Watson had finally succeeded in perfecting their device, which used a vibrating membrane made from thinly hammered metal. When a person spoke into the device, the sound waves of his or her voice would cause the membrane to vibrate up and down. In turn the membrane would send a continuous modulating electric current down a wire to a matching device with a vibrating membrane. The current coming down the wire would cause this second membrane to vibrate, recreating the sound wave of the spoken voice at the other end, thus allowing another person to hear that voice. At first Bell and Watson had managed to get their telephone working between two rooms in their workshop, but through repeated improvements in the device they were soon able to transmit their voices to each other a distance of two miles. Tom had to admit, it was a stunning achievement.

Tom also learned that Bell had offered to sell the patent for the telephone to Western Union, telling the company's president, William Orton, that the new system would one day replace the telegraph. But Orton had scoffed at this notion and passed on the opportunity to purchase Bell's patent. Instead Bell had started his own company, Bell Telephone.

On May 10, 1876, the Centennial Exposition in Philadelphia opened. This was the first exposition of its kind in the United States, and it was held to mark the one-hundredth anniversary of the signing of the Declaration of Independence. The exhibition site covered more than 450 acres of land, and people flocked to see the more than thirty thousand exhibits on display. The focal point of the show was Machinery Hall, where visitors could marvel at the various engineering wonders of the age, such as an elevator, locomotives, fire trucks, printing presses, mining equipment, and magic lanterns. Because Thomas Edison was one of the country's leading inventors, a number of his devices were on display there, including his quadruplexing equipment and the electric pen. Alexander Graham Bell's newly invented telephone was also on display. The device caused a sensation as people flocked to hear a human voice transmitted over wires.

The Centennial Exposition lasted for six months, during which time Tom got to work on other inventions in his new laboratory at Menlo Park. Even though he lived just a three-minute walk from the laboratory, he often became so involved in his work that he slept there, usually for an hour or two at a time.

Tom soon found the perfect spot for his naps. Beneath the stairwell was a storage cupboard into which Tom threw some old newspapers, turning the cupboard into his sleeping hideout. Tom never bothered to take off any of his clothes or shoes when he crawled in for a nap. He believed that taking off your clothes to sleep meant it was less likely that you would fall asleep. Even on the nights when he did manage to make it home, he liked to sleep with his clothes on.

While Tom liked living in the countryside at Menlo Park, Mary was not as enthusiastic. She tried hard to keep her city ways. She ordered most of the family's groceries from Park and Tilford in New York City, and she made regular trips to Lord and Taylor in Manhattan to buy new outfits. She employed three servants to help out around the house, and she kept them on a tight schedule cleaning and polishing the fashionable items that adorned the Edison home.

In the meantime, Tom learned from William Orton, who had initially scoffed at Bell's "far speaker" and had turned down the offer to purchase the patent for the device, that as the Centennial Exposition progressed, Western Union was growing concerned. The telephone on display there was causing such a public sensation that Western Union had changed its mind and wanted to buy Bell's patent. But now that Bell had established his own company to produce and market the telephone, he was no longer interested in selling his patent. This was bad news to Orton, who feared that Bell might have been right, that the telephone may indeed one day replace the telegraph. Orton told Tom that since Bell did not want to sell his patent, Western Union wanted Tom to produce an improved version of the device for the company to use. Such improvements, he explained, would allow Western Union to circumvent Bell's telephone patent.

Tom agreed to take on the project. In closely examining Bell's invention, he had noticed a number of improvements that could be made to it. In the fall of 1876 Tom and his crew began laboring away to improve the telephone.

The biggest improvement to be made, Tom noted, was to strengthen the electric current that was passed along the line from telephone to telephone. With Bell's phone it was not uncommon for a person to have to yell into it several times before the person's voice could be heard at the other end of the line, and even then the voice was not always particularly clear. And with his poor hearing, it was nearly impossible for Tom to hear anything over Bell's device. What was needed was a stronger transmitter that would deliver a clearer signal over a much greater distance than was presently possible.

For the next six months Tom kept busy testing the electrical properties of over two thousand different chemical compounds. Eventually his persistence paid off. Tom discovered that carbon would transmit a stronger signal. He scraped some carbon from the inside of a kerosene lantern and molded it into two small buttons. One of the buttons was attached to the diaphragm of the telephone, while the other button was set in close contact with the first button. Now when a person spoke into the phone and sound waves vibrated the diaphragm up and down, the two carbon buttons moved closer to or farther away from each other, varying the electric current that passed between them and in turn producing a much stronger signal to be passed along the wire to the telephone at the other end.

Now when Tom listened to the telephone, he could hear it loud and clear. Not only that, but the mushiness had gone from the sound so that he could clearly make out the vowels and consonants that made up each word spoken.

Soon, behind the laboratory, along the fence that ran around the Menlo Park compound, Tom had the carbon shed erected. Inside the shed were twelve kerosene lamps that were kept burning throughout the night. As the lamps burned and deposited carbon on the inside of the lamp chimney, the night watchman would scrape the carbon off at regular intervals and work it into a pastelike consistency. The watchman would then roll it into long noodles, which were sliced into three-hundred-millimeter-wide segments that formed the carbon buttons to use in the new, improved telephone.

In January 1877, as Tom was finishing up his improvements to Bell's telephone, the weather turned bitter cold as a fierce storm rolled across New Jersey. The wind blew so hard that for the laboratory not to be blown over, Tom had twenty old Western Union telegraph poles propped against its side. He then passed a restless night waiting to see whether his invention factory would stand up to the elements. Fortunately the building survived, and the next morning, with the temperature at five degrees below zero, Tom, bundled in his warmest overcoat, made his way to the laboratory. He found everything inside frozen, with many of the bottles and jars containing his chemicals and compounds cracked and broken. But rather than bemoan what had happened inside the lab, Tom saw it as a wonderful opportunity to study the properties of the chemicals and compounds in a state of extreme cold, something he had not had the opportunity to do before.

Tom set up his microscope in the chilly laboratory and set to work. He was fascinated by some of the discoveries he was making. But in his enthusiasm with the task, he became a little careless. He laid out a batch of sulfur chloride in a dish and took a beaker of water to dilute the compound. As he began pouring the water onto the sulfur, the mixture exploded, splattering his face and eyes with sulfur chloride. Tom dropped everything and ran for a water hydrant, where he let icy cold water wash over his face. The water helped to dilute the mixture, but it did little to take away the burning in his eyes. Tom's eyes were cloudy, and for the next three days Tom fretted that his sight might be permanently impaired, as was his hearing. Fortunately, as the days rolled on, the stinging stopped and the cloudiness in his eyes began to recede until Tom could see normally again, though it was two weeks before he could resume work in his laboratory.

As he worked on improving the telephone, Tom found his mind filled with ideas for future experiments. Where other men saw only the machine in their hands, Tom saw the gateway to many other developments. In the telephone he saw the seeds of a new machine that would be able to capture sound and store it until the operator chose to listen to it.

Tom kept the idea to himself and started experimenting. His experiments were built on the principles of sound vibration he had encountered in working with the telephone. But instead of using the vibration of a diaphragm to send an electric current down a wire, Tom hoped to store the unique pattern of those sound waves onto some kind of medium material from which, using another diaphragm, he hoped to reproduce the sound. Slowly, painstakingly, with the help of Charles Batchelor, Tom began to close in on the final design for his new invention, which he had already begun to refer to as the phonograph, made up from the Greek words for "sound" and "write."

The design was quite simple. A spiral-grooved brass cylinder, three and a half inches in diameter, was mounted onto a long, fixed screw that was turned by a hand crank. As the screw was cranked, the brass cylinder rotated and moved along the screw from right to left. Wrapped around the brass cylinder at precisely the right tension was a sheet of tinfoil. Mounted at the middle of the device was a diaphragm Tom had borrowed from the telephone. Attached directly to the diaphragm was a needle that floated minutely above the grooves in the brass cylinder but made contact with the tinfoil as the screw was turned and the cylinder passed under it. On the other side of the device was another diaphragm and needle.

If all went well and the invention actually worked, an operator would crank the handle while speaking into a funnel-like mouthpiece that housed one of the diaphragms. As this diaphragm vibrated in time to the sound waves from the operator's voice, it would leave a grooved pattern in the tinfoil. When the operator finished speaking, he would move the mouthpiece aside, wind the cylinder back to the beginning, and place the needle of the second diaphragm against the tinfoil. This time as the handle was cranked, the needle would run along the groove in the tinfoil and reproduce the sound of the operator's voice by causing the second diaphragm to vibrate and emit sound waves.

Eventually, in early December 1877, Tom sketched out the plans for his phonograph. He then asked John Kruesi to build the machine, though he did not tell him what exactly the machine was supposed to be used for. When John completed the phonograph on December 6, he asked Tom, "What is this machine for, anyway?"

"If all goes well, I might just be able to speak into it and have it repeat my words back to me later," Tom replied.

"Surely that's not possible from such a simple device," John countered, looking at the tinfoil wrapped around the cylinder.

"Well, let's see," Tom said.

Soon all of the workmen at Menlo Park were gathered around Tom's desk, with John positioned right in front of Tom. As Tom slowly began to turn the hand crank, he began shouting into the mouth-piece: "Mary had a little lamb, its fleece was white as snow."

The men waited anxiously for Tom to finish reciting the nursery rhyme. When he was done, Tom pulled the diaphragm and needle free from the tinfoil-encased cylinder, which he then wound back to the beginning. He adjusted the second diaphragm and needle against the tinfoil and once again began to crank the handle. This time, as Tom cranked, the words "Mary had a little lamb, its fleece was white as snow" emerged from the machine.

At the end of the nursery rhyme, the men stood in stunned silence. John let out an exclamation in German, "Mein Gott in himmel!" and then a cheer went up from everyone present.

Thomas Edison had invented the phonograph. He was truly the "Wizard of Menlo Park," as the press soon dubbed him.

Chapter 10

A Bright Idea

"A WONDERFUL INVENTION—SPEECH CAPABLE OF INDEFINITE REPETITION FROM AUTOMATIC RECORDS!" The blazing headline in *Scientific American* magazine was referring to Tom's invention of the phonograph. Meanwhile the *North American Review* wrote an essay titled "The Phonograph and Its Future." In the essay Tom was quoted about the possibilities that his new invention held. These included recording dictation, reading books aloud for the blind, teaching elocution, singing children to sleep, preserving the voices and words of great men, providing recorded music for music boxes and the voice for talking dolls, and for clocks that could tell a person the hour of the day.

Of course a device that could record a human voice and play it back at any time was almost impossible for most people to imagine, much less fathom how it actually worked. Still, many reporters tried to describe for their readers just how the device worked, some more successfully than others. This led the American humor magazine *Puck* to satirize these reporters' efforts to describe the phonograph. "You do not know what the Phonograph is?" the parody began. "Well, Puck will tell you. A quadruplex, double-driving, osculatory cog-wheel, gyrating in a fluted pedestal by the positive and negative current from a cautery voltaic battery strikes the atmospheric tympanic diaphragm. The rheotone depending on the vibratory armature of the secondary coil produces dynamic Faradization. Ahem!"

With the news of the invention of the phonograph, reporters and dignitaries began descending on Menlo Park, which it was rumored would soon be renamed "Edisonville." In a canny blend of showmanship and feigned bewilderment as to why they would seek him out, Tom welcomed these people to his laboratory and showed them around. No tour of the Menlo Park complex was complete without a demonstration of the electric pen, and of course the phonograph, which he hoped to produce and mass-market for one hundred dollars each.

It was not long before Tom was summoned to Washington, D.C., to show off his new invention to a gathering of the National Academy of Sciences. Upon his arrival in Washington, Tom was taken to photographer Mathew Brady's studio where he posed with the phonograph. While in Washington, Tom was invited to the Capitol to demonstrate the phonograph to a throng of fascinated members of Congress. Tom also gave a private demonstration of the device to Senators Beck and Blackburn. For this demonstration he cranked the phonograph while Senator Beck recited a poem by Scottish poet Robert Burns. When Tom played the recording back, the senator was astonished by what he heard. But to make sure that the device had really recorded his voice and that Tom was not playing some ventriloquist's trick on him, Senator Beck had Tom leave the room while he operated the phonograph himself. This seemed to satisfy him that the phonograph had in fact recorded his voice.

At eleven o'clock that evening Tom received word that President Hayes wanted a demonstration of the phonograph. So Tom set out for the White House, arriving there around midnight. The president welcomed Tom warmly and had his wife roused from her bed to come and hear the demonstration. President and Mrs. Hayes were absolutely fascinated by the phonograph and having their voices recorded and played back. In fact, they would not let Tom leave the White House until three-thirty in the morning.

While Tom was busy promoting the phonograph, business opportunities for him in England and Europe began to grow. In May 1878, Tom's nephew Charley convinced his uncle to send him to England with six of Tom's latest telephone receivers, which he planned to sell to the company with the highest bid. At first Tom was reluctant to send Charley, who was only eighteen years old. But since Tom had no doubts that Charley knew more about the receivers than anyone else, eventually he relented and sent his nephew on his way.

A couple of months later, Tom was off on his own adventure. He stood at the railway station at Menlo Park waiting for a train to take him west—way out west. Two professors, George Barker and Henry Draper, had invited Tom to accompany them to Rawlins, Wyoming, to observe an eclipse of the sun on July 29, 1878, and Tom had accepted. Tom planned to carry out an experiment to try to measure the temperature of the sun during an eclipse.

The moment the train pulled out of the station at Menlo Park with Tom aboard, Tom felt his spirits rise. Ever since he was a small child in Milan, Ohio, watching settlers and prospectors heading west in their wagons to catch the end of the California gold rush, he had felt the pull of the West. Now he was on his way in that direction, and his spirits continued to rise at every stop along the way. At many of these stops the local telegraphers would hail him as some kind of hero.

Following the eclipse of the sun, Tom and the two professors continued journeying westward, visiting Virginia City, riding bronco ponies, sleeping under the stars, and exploring silver mines. During this leg of the trip Tom was thrilled to be given permission to travel at the front of the train—not in the front carriage but right at the front of the locomotive, sitting atop the cowcatcher (the metal grill apron that stuck out from the front of the engine). He borrowed a cushion to sit on and wedged himself in tightly for the ride of a lifetime. The wind beat against his face as the train rolled along, and all the smoke and steam from the engine was behind him, leaving him with an uninterrupted view of the West.

The trio finally made it all the way to San Francisco, where they enjoyed all that the bustling city had to offer. As they made their way to San Francisco, Tom and the professors had spent many hours discussing the future of electricity and, in particular, the possibility of making a practical electric lightbulb.

By the time Tom arrived back at Menlo Park on August 26, 1878, his mind was fixed on one thing and one thing only—the electric light. "The electric light is the light of the future—and it will be my light, unless some other fellow gets up a better one," Tom told his men at Menlo Park. The race to produce the electric light was on. Tom then ordered that signs declaring "Positively No Admittance" be posted on all the doors to the laboratory and on the fence that surrounded the Menlo Park compound. Reporters and members of the public were no longer welcome to drop in at any time to see what Tom was up to. Work on producing a viable lightbulb was to be carried out in secret.

The month after arriving back from the trip west, Professor Barker arranged for Tom and some of his men to visit the Ansonia Brass and Clock Works in Connecticut. The owner of the Brass and Clock Works was a man named William Wallace, who four years before had built the first dynamo in America. This device turned mechanical energy into an electric current. In his factory Wallace had set up a series of eight electric arc lights that were powered by a telemachon, an electric generator connected to a water-powered turbine.

Tom, accompanied by George Barker, Charles Batchelor, and several other men from Menlo Park, arrived at the factory on Sunday, September 8. The trip was to prove pivotal in Tom's thinking about the development of electric lighting.

William Wallace greeted the visitors and shook Tom's hand warmly. He then proceeded to demonstrate his dynamo for the group. This was the first time that Tom had ever seen electric current delivered by any means other than a battery. Tom was greatly impressed, so impressed, in fact, that he ordered two of the dynamos for his lab in Menlo Park, where he intended to use them to provide the power he needed for his experiments with the electric lightbulb.

Following the demonstration of the dynamo, Wallace showed the guests his eight electric arc lights. The lights were wired together in what was called a series circuit. Electric current flowed to the first light and lit it, and then the current flowed from the first light to the second, and so on until a single electric current had lit all eight arc lights. The only problem with this approach was that all of the lights had to be on at once, and if one of the lamps went out, the circuit was broken, and all of the lights would go out.

As Tom silently walked around observing Wallace's lighting system, he realized that such a wiring scheme would never do in a house, where a homeowner would not necessarily need or want all of the lights on at once. And a system where all of the lights went out if one of the bulbs failed could become very frustrating to the owner as he scrambled about in the dark to rectify the problem. Tom realized that if electric lights were to become a reality in houses, he would need to come up with not only an effective lightbulb but also a better form of circuitry to supply power to the lights so that they would not all have to be on at once. He was still pondering this problem as he caught the train back to Menlo Park at the end of his visit with William Wallace.

Following his return from the Ansonia Brass and Clock Works, Tom began to be concerned about his wife's condition. Mary was prone to emotional outbursts, and she was growing unusually large, even for a woman seven and a half months pregnant. She, too, was worried about how big the unborn child seemed to be getting. And she had good cause to be alarmed. When William Leslie Edison was born on October 26, 1878, he arrived in the world weighing in at a hefty twelve pounds. Tom was glad to have another son, and he was glad that Mary's pregnancy was over. Now that the child had been born, Tom could turn all of his attention back to the electric lightbulb.

As he got back to work on building an efficient lightbulb, Tom was able to draw on the experiments that other inventors had performed. He knew that his light would contain a filament set in a vacuum in a glass globe. The real challenge was finding the right filament. Other than that, the principle of the lightbulb was fairly straightforward. A current was passed through a narrow filament of a material that had high resistance to the current passing through it. This resistance created heat, which in turn caused the filament to glow, or become incandescent, and give off light. However, if a substance became incandescent in the presence of oxygen, it would quickly burn up, hence the need to place the filament in a vacuum.

Tom started experimenting with a number of different metals to use as a filament for his light. Eventually he settled on platinum, a metal that had a high melting point. During his experiments Tom was able to get a strand of platinum inside a glass bulb to glow brightly.

While Tom was experimenting in his laboratory at Menlo Park, his friend Grosvenor Lowrey was hard at work on his behalf. Lowrey was general counsel for Western Union as well as Tom's legal and financial adviser. While Tom was busy working on the lightbulb, Lowrey was busy gathering a group of investors together to support Tom's latest venture. It was not long before Lowrey informed Tom of his success in bringing together the investors. In October 1878 the Edison Electric Light Company was founded.

Tom was delighted with the infusion of money he received from his investors. Not only would the money free him to keep experimenting at perfecting the lightbulb, it would also allow him to focus on the next step, providing electricity to run the lightbulbs once they were installed in peoples' homes. Tom had already come up with the concept of the parallel circuit, which avoided the problem he had noted on his visit to the Ansonia Brass and Clock Works where Wallace had his arc lights wired in a series circuit. The concept of the parallel circuit was modeled on the gas pipes that fed the gaslights installed in many of the homes and offices in large cities like New York. In that case a number of small gas lines branched out from the main gas line that carried gas into a house. Each of these branch lines was connected to an individual gaslight, so that all the lights in a house or office could be operated independently of one another. Tom pictured the same for his electric lights, where wires branched from a single power cable to feed current to individual lights, allowing them to work independently of one another.

Of course the next question was, Where was the electricity to run the lights going to come from in the first place? To come up with the answer to this question, Tom used the same analogy of the gas lines. The gas was brought to houses from the gasworks through large pipes installed under the city streets, and the gas lines into the individual houses branched off from these main gas lines. So why not do the same with electricity? Why not set up a plant to house large dynamos capable of producing a lot of electricity. This electricity could then be carried to houses through cables laid under the streets like the gas pipes. So while Tom carried on his experiments with the lightbulb, he began work on making this concept a reality. He began designing and having his men build bigger and better electric generators.

In the meantime Tom's experiments with the electric lightbulb dragged on. Although platinum worked as a filament in the bulb, Tom could not keep the filament incandescent for more than a few minutes before it burned out. Tom decided that he needed a better pump to create the vacuum inside the bulb. He ordered a Sprengel pump from England. Once the pump arrived and was set up, sure enough, it created a much better vacuum inside the bulb. This in turn allowed the platinum filament to burn longer and brighter, though still not long enough to be commercially viable. Tom had also discovered that the thinner the filament, the brighter its incandescent glow.

After a year of working on the lightbulb, Tom was still unhappy with the results. He had managed to extend the life of the platinum filament considerably, but not enough. And despite testing thousands of other metals and combinations of metals, he had not come up with a replacement for platinum. To make matters worse, even if he did succeed at getting a platinum filament to burn for an acceptable length of time, Tom learned that platinum was not a plentiful metal, and so the cost of a lightbulb with a platinum filament would not be as cheap as he had hoped. There had to be a better material for the filament, but what was it?

In the midst of pondering this question, Tom received some bad news from Europe regarding Charley. It seemed that Charley had made his way to

Paris against Tom's orders and had set himself up in a wild lifestyle there. But before Tom could think of a way to reel his wayward nephew back into the family fold, Charley became very ill. Despite the best medical care available in Paris, which included leeches and laxatives, Charley died on October 19, 1879, at nineteen years of age. His death was a severe blow to the Edison clan. Tom paid the three-thousand-dollar debt that Charley had accumulated. He also paid to have Charley's body embalmed in Paris and then shipped back home to Port Huron, Michigan, for burial. Tom did not attend the funeral. His excuse was that he was too busy with his work to take the time to trek to Port Huron. In truth, Tom did not like being around emotional displays, which he was sure his nephew's funeral would be.

In his search for a better filament, Tom finally decided to turn his attention to something that was in plentiful supply around the laboratory—carbon. After doing some experiments and calculations, Tom decided that a carbon filament one sixty-fourth of an inch thick was what he needed. Soon the men in the laboratory were kneading carbon mixed with tar, a process that took several hours. Then they did their best to roll the mixture out into thin strands for the filaments. This was not an easy process, and Tom and Charles Batchelor looked for a better way to produce the filaments. They settled on carbonizing (that is, partially burning a substance in a furnace) lengths of cotton thread.

Finally Tom produced a carbonized filament that Charles, with steady hands, carefully loaded into a bulb. The air was sucked out to create a vacuum, and current was applied to the filament. Tom and the other men in the lab watched intently as the carbonized filament became incandescent. Then they waited to see how long the filament would burn. The two hours that the platinum filament had burned came and went, and still the carbonized filament glowed. Finally, after thirteen and a half hours, it burned out. Tom was ecstatic.

The next day Tom produced another filament, and he and the other men tried the experiment once again. This time the filament glowed incandescent for forty hours. Tom sat quietly after the filament burned out while the men around him celebrated, clapping each other on the back and saying, "We've got it!"

Finally a thoughtful Thomas Edison looked up. "If it can burn for that number of hours, I know I can make it burn a hundred hours," he declared.

More experiments followed, until on November 1, 1879, Tom applied for a patent for the incandescent, carbon filament lamp. He noted in the filing that the best filament had been produced from carbonizing strips of Bristol cardboard to hairlike strands. He had been able to get these filaments to burn for 170 hours.

Now it was time for Tom to show the world his achievement.

Chapter 11

The Best Lights Ever

Tom had several more problems to overcome with the lightbulb, but by December 20, he felt confident enough to allow his friend, journalist Edwin Fox, to release an article he had been writing about the electric lightbulb. The following day, Sunday, December 21, 1879, the *New York Herald* newspaper devoted its entire front page to the story. "The Great Inventor's Triumph in Electric Illumination," the headline declared, lauding the newly invented lightbulb as "a bright, beautiful light, like the mellow sunset of an Italian autumn. A light that is a little globe of sunshine, a veritable Aladdin's lamp."

Publication of the article in the *Herald* was timed to coincide with a lavish display of electric lighting that Tom had planned. Tom installed lights in the laboratory at Menlo Park, the railroad station, and the houses in the village, and he even slung lights outside between the buildings. Because he had not yet invented a system to switch the lights on and off, he rigged a single telegraph key to control them all.

On December 31, 1879, the lights of Menlo Park—all eighty of them—were turned on in a public exhibition. Three thousand people poured into Menlo Park, eager to see the new wonder of the electric lightbulb. They marveled at the soft, white aura of the lights that glowed in the snowy night and illuminated the parlors of houses. Visitors to the village trampled plants and broke laboratory equipment in their enthusiasm to catch a glimpse of the man who had made all that they were seeing possible. Eventually Tom clambered onto a ladder so that he could be seen above the throng.

When daylight finally broke, those who had come to see the display of the electric lightbulb were true believers. They had no doubt that they had witnessed the dawn of a new era. But many people who had not seen the display scoffed at electric lighting. One "expert" in electricity noted, "One must have lost all recollection of American hoaxes to accept such claims. The sorcerer of Menlo Park appears not to be acquainted with the subtleties of the electrical science. Mr. Edison takes us backwards." And another so-called expert wrote that Thomas Edison's experiments were a fraud.

Tom, though, was much too busy to be concerned about such reports. He knew he had invented something wonderful, and his next job was to produce an electric generating system that was sturdy, cheap, and convenient enough to light up New York City with electric lights. This was a huge challenge, and Tom did his best to prepare people for the possibility that it would be a long, slow task to set up. He wrote,

> There is a wide difference between completing an invention and putting the manufactured article on the market. The public, especially the public of journalism, stubbornly refuse to recognize this difference. It was years after photography was invented before the first photograph was taken; years after the steamboat and telegraph were invented before they were actually set going. George Stephenson built his first locomotive ten years before he made his *Rocket* run from Liverpool to Manchester, and he and Robert Fulton were called fool, charlatan, fraud, lunatic—everything [people] could think of. [People] demanded that he should "hurry up," or acknowledge himself a humbug.

Despite Tom's best efforts to temper people's expectations, many believed that Tom had worked a miracle in producing the electric lightbulb and it would now be simple for him to reproduce that miracle over and over. They seemed to lose sight of the fact that electric lightbulbs needed a steady supply of electricity on which to run and that the next part of making electric lighting in homes a reality was developing a generation and distribution system for electricity.

In the lab at Menlo Park, Tom and his crew worked around the clock perfecting the lightbulb. Once again the laboratory was closed to the public, and within three weeks Tom had managed to stretch the lifespan of a lightbulb to 550 hours.

Then for a while Tom laid aside his plans to light up New York City and concentrated on a smaller-scale demonstration of electric lights at work. He agreed to install electric lighting on a new 3,200-ton steamship named the *Columbia,* which was being built in Chester, Pennsylvania. In mid-April 1880 the ship sailed from Chester into New York Harbor and anchored at the foot of Wall Street to be fitted out with electric lights. Four steam-powered dynamos were installed in the ship, and then wires were run along the corridors and lights installed in individual cabins and the public areas of the ship. The lightbulbs stood upright in wooden holders and were held in place by gravity. The switches for the individual lights were in locked metal boxes outside the cabins and could only be turned on and off by a steward.

When the lights were turned on for the first time, the sight of the *Columbia* at anchor in the dark harbor lit by glowing electric lights created quite a stir. People flocked to the shoreline for a closer look at the amazing sight.

Ten days after the lights were fitted, the *Columbia* sailed out of New York Harbor bound for Portland, Oregon. Lighting the ship proved to be a brilliant publicity stunt. On its way to Portland, the *Columbia* made stops at Rio de Janeiro, Brazil; Valparaiso, Chile; and San Francisco, California. And as Tom had hoped, at each of these ports of call the sight of a ship lit by electric lightbulbs caused a flurry of excitement and generated hundreds of newspaper reports. The electric lightbulb had captured the world's imagination.

Tom was still using carbonized strips of Bristol cardboard as the filaments for his lightbulbs, but he was growing frustrated with the material. The carbonized Bristol filaments were brittle and prone to breaking during production, causing the manufacture of lightbulbs to be a slow and laborious process in which the successful production of three bulbs was considered a good day's work. The filaments also tended to deposit a carbon residue on the inside of the bulb after a few hours' use, greatly reducing the amount of light emitted. Tom continued to search for a better filament, carbonizing all manner of things, from grasses and mosses to coconut palms, palmettos, and hemp. He even tried carbonizing hairs from John Kruesi's beard. But none of these proved to be better filaments than the Bristol board.

On Friday, July 9, 1880, Tom was sitting in the lab at Menlo Park pondering the problem of a better filament when he noticed a bamboo fan lying on one of the workbenches. This wasn't the first time he had seen the fan. The bamboo fan had been used to hurry along the process of evaporation during chemical experiments, but this time when he saw it, Tom began to wonder how carbonized bamboo would work as a filament. He cut a narrow strip of bamboo from the fan and had it carbonized and sealed in a bulb. The following day he applied power to the bulb, and the carbonized bamboo began to glow. Tom was delighted, and after six weeks of further experiments, he was convinced that he had found the right material for his filaments. The carbonized bamboo did not suffer the same weaknesses as the Bristol board, and it would burn for hundreds of hours.

Of course developing an electric supply system, along with manufacturing lightbulbs, was a huge task, and throughout 1880 Tom's facility at Menlo Park began to grow. New workers were employed and new buildings were erected to house the various facets of the operation, such as producing new and bigger generators.

Tom decided that before he began to install an electric supply system in New York City, he needed to know how the system would work. In the fields beside his Menlo Park laboratory he laid out an imaginary grid representing the streets of New York. Then his men got busy digging shallow trenches in which to bury the underground cables. The cables would in turn supply electricity from a generator to scores of lightbulbs mounted on poles.

Before the cables were laid in the trenches, they had to be insulated. Tom decided that wood would make a good insulator for the cables, and grooved boards were first laid in the trenches and then the wires were placed inside the grooves. The trenches were then covered over with six inches of dirt, and hundreds of wooden posts were installed, each one supporting a single lightbulb. By July 20, 1880, everything was ready for a test of the system.

Tom wanted to try the new system on a wet day to see how well it would function in the rain. Several days later rain swept in across the New Jersey countryside, and Tom declared it a perfect day for the test. The steam engine that would power the generator was fired up. When everything was ready, Tom gave the word. The generator began to spin and feed electricity out to the underground cables. That was when things started to go wrong. The lights barely flickered because they were receiving so little electricity. This was because wood turned out not to be a good insulator after all. In fact, so much electricity was leaking from the wires into the ground that everything around the test site, including the trees, was charged with electricity. This was not the outcome Tom had been expecting, and he ordered the generator shut down and the cables dug up. He obviously had to find a better insulator for his wires, but what was it?

Tom sent his assistant Wilson Howell to the library to research everything that had been written about the subject of insulation and report back to him in two weeks. With the results of Wilson's search in hand, Tom undertook another series of experiments to test the electrical insulating qualities of a number of various compounds. As a result of these experiments, Tom settled on a mixture of Trinidad asphalt mixed with linseed oil and small amounts of paraffin and beeswax. The foul-smelling concoction was cooked up in 250-gallon kettles, and then strips of muslin were dunked into the mixture and then wrapped around the wires.

Ten boys were paid to carry out the dirty work, and they soon found that despite its smell, once it cooled, the mixture made a good chewing gum. Land turtles, too, seemed to like chewing on the formula and quickly became a nuisance. They would crawl over each other as they "raced" to get to the newly insulated wires. Some days the boys doing the insulating would pull twenty or more turtles from the small junction boxes located along the cable before they could begin their day's work.

Finally, on November 1, 1880, the electric supply system was ready to be tried once again. This time the test was a success. The electrical current traveled along the insulated wires and lit the lightbulbs perched on the posts. Satisfied with the test, on November 20 Tom sent a representative to New York City to begin negotiating with the city council for the right to install electric cables under the city streets.

At the same time Tom converted the electric pen facility at Menlo Park into a factory to produce lightbulbs. More than one hundred men were hired to manufacture the bulbs. The bulbs were purchased in two halves, the filament was inserted, and then the two halves were fused together. Finally a glass plug was used to seal the bottom of the bulb. Alcohol was used to make the seal between the glass plug and the bulb airtight. Tom soon realized, however, that the supply of alcohol was going down suspiciously fast. He ordered the factory manager to dye the alcohol green. From then on, any man caught with green-tinged lips was fired on the spot.

With his focus now clearly on lighting New York City, in March 1881 Tom rented a four-story brownstone house located at 65 Fifth Avenue to serve as his New York headquarters. The house was located in a fashionable part of town, and Tom had a giant sign hung outside the place. The sign, which read "Edison Electric Light Co.," was designed to remind the rich and famous of New York that electric light was on the way.

Soon afterward the lamp factory moved from Menlo Park into a fire-damaged complex of buildings just outside Newark that Tom purchased for a bargain price. Numerous unemployed families were living nearby the new factory, and children especially were recruited to work there because of the very low wages they could be paid.

The lamp factory was not the only thing that moved from Menlo Park. The machine shop at Menlo Park was dismantled and transferred to the old Roach Iron Works on Goerck Street in New York. From then on, Tom and many of his key workers spent most of their time in New York City overseeing operations there.

Tom still had many problems to overcome before the installation of electric lights and the power supply system in New York could go ahead. Steam engines had to be improved so that they could spin the generators much faster. As a result Tom engaged the services of Charles Porter, one of America's best steam engineers, to design the new steam engines. Also, the electric lightbulbs were easily knocked out of their wooden sockets, since they relied on gravity to hold them in place. The answer to this problem came one night in Tom's workshop. As Tom unscrewed a can of kerosene to clean his hands, one of his men made a startling suggestion. "Why don't we make the bottom of the bulb into a screw and screw it into the socket. Then it wouldn't come out if it was knocked."

The idea was brilliantly simple, one that Tom wished he had thought of himself. The screw-mounted bulbs worked perfectly. And since the bulbs were no longer dependent on gravity to hold them in place, they could be mounted upside down from the ceiling, allowing them to cast their light over a greater area.

Of course, no one had ever tried to wire a building for electric light before, and men had to be trained to handle the task, though at first most of their training came in the form of learning from the mistakes they made. Wooden floorboards had to be pulled up and electric wires inserted beneath them. As the men soon learned, if this was not done correctly, the floor could catch fire.

Progress on setting up the system in New York was slow, and Tom decided to break his dream of lighting the city with electric lights into smaller chunks. He started by lighting the Edison Electric Light Company headquarters at 65 Fifth Avenue. Wires were run throughout the house, and sockets and lightbulbs were installed, along with a small steam-powered dynamo to supply the needed power. Once this building was lit with electric lightbulbs, hundreds of people would come by every night to see the sight. Soon other buildings—including hotels; cotton, wool, and silk mills; piano factories; homes; and offices—were wired for electric light. Each of these installations had its own steam-powered dynamo to supply the power for the lights. "Lighting fever" was catching on fast.

In August 1881 the Paris Electrical Exhibition was to be held in Paris, France, followed in January 1882 by the Crystal Palace Exhibition in London, England. Tom intended to display his electric light system at both exhibitions. He dispatched Charles Batchelor to France to plan the display in Paris. Another associate, Edward Johnson, was charged with setting up the display in London. The Thomas Edison electric light display at both shows won hands down over more primitive lighting systems that the Europeans and English were working on. In fact the response to the displays was so great that subsidiaries of the Edison Electric Light Company were established in France and England.

Soon orders for electric light installations were pouring in from across Europe. Electric light systems were installed in the opera house in Vienna, Austria; a sugar refinery in Antwerp, Belgium; a porcelain factory in Lorraine, France; and the Galleria shopping arcade in Milan, Italy.

Tom and his electric lights had won the hearts and minds of the public the world over, but Tom had still not been able to make good on his promise to light New York City. The task was bigger and more costly than even he had imagined. Tom decided to scale back his plans to the lighting of just fifty square blocks of the city, an area equal to one-sixth of a square mile. The area he settled on lighting was bordered by the East River to the east, Wall Street to the south, Nassau Street to the west, and Spruce Street to the north. Although this area did not contain a lot of residential buildings, it did incorporate most of the city's financial district. Tom was eager to demonstrate his system to men who might be interested in investing in his company, especially since setting up an electric supply system was turning out to be much more expensive than he had first imagined.

A three-story, double-wide building at 255–257 Pearl Street was purchased to serve as the generating plant for the system. Renovations on the building began immediately, opening up the building's interior and strengthening it so that it could support the weight and vibrations of the boilers, steam engines, and heavy generators that would be installed in the structure.

Then the cables had to be laid from the new power plant on Pearl Street to feed power to the buildings in the area. This proved to be a great challenge. The city council set strict limits on when Tom's men could work on the project—from eight at night until four in the morning. Tom had a small steam engine, dynamo, and electric arc lights installed on a wagon, and the contraption provided light for the men to work by.

Tom himself loved to work alongside the men as they dug trenches, laid insulated copper cable under the streets, and then ran branch cables alongside the gas pipes into the various buildings. Slowly, ever so slowly, the project was coming together.

In early 1882, as cables were being laid under the city streets, household matters caught up with Tom. Mary had never fully recovered her health after the birth of William a little over three years before. Now the doctor informed Tom that Mary was so ill, both mentally and physically, that he was afraid she might die. Tom agreed to leave the ongoing cable installation work in New York and accompany Mary and the three children on a vacation to Green Cove, near St. Augustine, Florida. The Edison family spent two months at Green Cove, and when they returned, Mary was feeling a little better. Upon their return to New York, Tom moved his family into a suite at the Clarendon Hotel, across the street from the Edison Electric Light Company house on Fifth Avenue.

With his family settled in at the Clarendon, Tom went back to work. He had to get some part of the New York skyline lit up with electric lights. So far he had spent $480,000 on the project and had few results to show for it. Shares in his lighting company had fallen drastically, and he was losing the public's confidence that he could in fact get the job done.

Finally things began to come together. By June the Pearl Street power station was ready to supply electricity, and by August all the cables had been laid and light fixtures installed in houses and buildings. Finally, at three in the afternoon on Monday, September 4, 1882, a delighted and relieved Thomas Edison gave the order to his chief electrician at the power station to throw the main switch. Immediately the lights in forty buildings, eight hundred lightbulbs in all, went on. Of course it was not until darkness descended over the city that people fully began to appreciate Tom's achievement. "I have accomplished all that I promised," a triumphant Tom declared.

But there was still work to be done. There was an ongoing problem with the governors in the power station that meant only one of the six installed generators could run at a time. Also, more wires and light fixtures had to be installed in buildings throughout the area. And Tom did not yet have a way of measuring how much electricity each building was using. For the time being, the power was free, but Tom did not care too much. With forty buildings now lit with electric lights, New York was seeing a glimpse of what the future held, and Thomas Edison had proved he could deliver that future.

One of those who watched the lights come on that day was a young Croatian named Nikola Tesla. Nikola was tall and gaunt and gave the impression of being slightly mad, but he was a genius when it came to electricity. Charles Batchelor had sent Nikola to Tom from Europe, and Tom put the young man to work building dynamos and electric motors. Nikola had a deep and intuitive understanding of the nature of electricity and, in particular, of the theory of rotating magnetic fields. He had tried to talk to Tom about this theory and how it might be employed to improve Tom's system of generating and distributing electricity, but Tom had dismissed Nikola's ideas as impractical.

Little did Tom know that day as he basked in the glory of forty buildings aglow with incandescent electric lights that in five years Nikola Tesla's "impractical" ideas would be embraced by George Westinghouse, who would become Tom's greatest competitor in the business of generating and distributing electric power, and would give Westinghouse's company the edge in that race.

Sadly, Mary's health problems were not solved by the trip to St. Augustine, and in February 1884 Tom took her on another trip to Green Cove. This time, though, the trip did Mary little good. As a result, when the family returned to the Edisons' fashionable new home at 25 Gramercy Park, Tom had to hire a strong, male nurse to care for his wife. Still it was a shock to Tom when in early August Mary complained of a splitting headache. The doctor was called, and he diagnosed her condition as congestion of the brain. On August 9, 1884, Mary Stilwell Edison died at age twenty-nine. At thirty-seven years of age, Thomas Edison was a widower with three young children to care for.

Chapter 12

Mina

W e're off to New Orleans!" twelve-year-old Dot Edison exclaimed. "What will it be like? Will there be alligators in the Mississippi like there are in Florida?"

Tom was not sure of the answer to his daughter's questions, and he knew that he would not have time to explore the creatures of the Mississippi River anyway. He had been careful to keep as busy as possible in the six months since Mary's death. Now he was on his way to the World Industrial and Cotton Centennial Exposition in New Orleans, to be held from December 1884 to May 1885. The Edison Electric Light Company had assembled at the New Orleans exposition the world's largest incandescent lighting plant, which illuminated all 250 acres of buildings and fairgrounds. The exposition was so named because it had been one hundred years since the first cotton was exported from the United States. But while the exposition was being held in honor of cotton, it had turned into a world exhibition of the newest technologies, horticultural practices, and cultures.

In addition to lighting the exposition, Tom had another reason for visiting the show. He had recently negotiated a contract with the American Bell Telephone Company by which the company agreed to pay him twelve thousand dollars a year for five years to continue experimenting with ways to improve the telephone. The Bell Company had a booth at the World Industrial and Cotton Centennial Exposition where it was displaying some of Tom's telephone equipment.

The new arrangement with the American Bell Telephone Company had also brought Tom back in contact with his old friend Ezra Gilliland, who was head of the company's Experimental Department in Boston. As a result, the two men had decided to attend the exposition together. They also had decided that afterward, rather than return immediately to the snowy Northeast they would travel to St. Augustine, Florida, to do some hunting.

Tom arrived in New Orleans on February 28, 1885, two weeks after his thirty-eighth birthday. Daughter Dot accompanied him, while the two boys stayed behind with their grandmother Stilwell. The weather during the trip to New Orleans was cold and rainy, and Tom was glad to be traveling. He remembered back to the last time he had visited New Orleans, nearly twenty years before. Back then he had been planning to move to Brazil to work as a telegraph operator, but things had not worked out for him to leave. Now, as the train rumbled along on its way to New Orleans, Tom pondered how much things had changed for him in the years since.

Ezra and his wife, Lillian, were already in New Orleans, and Tom contacted them on his arrival in the city. In his newly single state, Tom valued the renewed friendship with Ezra, and the two men reminisced about the Civil War days when they were telegraph operators together in Adrian, Michigan, and roommates in Cincinnati.

Of course Tom had lots of other things to do at the exposition besides reminisce. He inspected the lighting setup and made sure that everything was operating as it should. And since Tom was America's foremost inventor, people flocked to make his acquaintance. While Tom was busy tweaking the lighting system and talking to people, Dot wandered through the exposition buildings, reporting back to her father the breathless tales of what she had seen: Chinese pagodas and the Liberty Bell, which had been specially sent from Philadelphia for the occasion.

Strangely, while Tom was surrounded by all manner of amazing technological innovations at the exposition, it was a certain young woman named Mina Miller who captured his attention. Mina was the nineteen-year-old daughter of Lewis Miller, a rich and respected farm-implement manufacturer from Akron, Ohio.

The Millers and the Gillilands were old friends, and Tom was soon drawn into their social circle. He would often sit in the parlor of the Millers' rented house in New Orleans and listen as Mina played the piano and recited poems. Tom was smitten with Mina's polished performances and her dark, exotic looks. Before long he had set his mind to courting Mina. Tom realized that he would have to proceed slowly, though, at least for him. Because Mina would be leaving New Orleans soon to return to finishing school in Boston, Tom decided to make plans to visit her and her large family of nine brothers and sisters in Akron, Ohio, as soon as possible.

At the end of the World Industrial and Cotton Centennial Exposition, Tom dispatched Dot back to New York, and Ezra's wife returned to Boston. The two men then set out for St. Augustine. It was an unusually cold winter, even in Florida, and finding St. Augustine too cold, Tom and Ezra ventured farther south by train and then by yacht, until they arrived at Fort Myers on the southwest Florida coast. They booked into the only hotel in the place, and Tom set out to explore the area.

Fort Myers was a tiny, bustling town of fifty inhabitants. It boasted a church, a livery stable, several stores, and its own newspaper. The town's streets were unpaved, and it seemed to Tom that more alligators, deer, and flamingoes were on the road than people. Tropical vegetation abounded everywhere: thirty-foot-tall orange trees along with bananas, pineapples, bamboo, sugar cane, and coconuts. There was also an abundance of wild turkeys and deer and an array of amazingly colorful birds.

Within two days of arriving in Fort Myers, Tom had purchased a thirteen-acre plot of land in the town, land suitable for building a summerhouse and laboratory on. He offered half of the land to Ezra so that the two friends could have adjacent homes and share the laboratory. Now that he owned land in Fort Myers, Tom ordered a prefabricated house from Maine to be shipped to the site and assembled, and he started sketching layouts for the gardens.

Once he was back in New York City, Tom tried to concentrate on inventing, but he could not seem to get Mina Miller out of his mind. In June Tom accepted an invitation to spend a week at Woodside Villa, the Gillilands' beachside home outside Boston. Tom was delighted when he arrived there and found that Mina was among the houseguests. Tom's infatuation with her grew.

Then in August Tom accepted an invitation to speak at the Literary and Scientific Circle at Chautauqua, a small village in western New York State. The village had been established a decade earlier as a camp to train Sunday-school workers and had grown into a fashionable cultural summer vacation destination for wealthy Protestants. The village had been the brainchild of Mina's father, Lewis Miller, and John Vincent, a bishop in the Methodist Church.

Miller had fronted most of the money to get the place started, as he and his wife were devout and generous Methodists.

The religious atmosphere that Mina had been raised in did not daunt Tom, who had little time for religion, and Tom determined to make a good impression on her family. He got on particularly well with Mina's older brother Ira, since they were both interested in mining iron ore and in a magnetic ore separator.

On August 21, 1885, a small group including the Gillilands, Mina, and Tom decided to visit Mount Washington, the highest point in the northeastern United States, located in the White Mountains of New Hampshire. Finally Tom and Mina could spend some uninterrupted time together.

Tom wanted to have private conversations with Mina, but because he was hard of hearing, people had to speak loudly around him so that he could hear what they said. Not wanting everyone around to hear his private conversations with Mina, he employed a different form of communication with her. He taught her Morse code, and then he tapped what he wanted to say into her hand, and she tapped her reply back on his hand. This proved to be a great way to communicate.

By the time the weeklong adventure to Mount Washington was over, Tom was confident that the time would soon be right to ask Mina Miller to marry him.

In September Mina once again came to visit the Gillilands, and Tom took the opportunity to visit her at Woodside Villa. During the visit he tapped out a question on Mina's hand: "Will you marry me?"

Without flinching, Mina tapped back her answer: "Yes!"

Tom was enough of a strategist to realize that only half the battle was over. He was a thirty-eight-year-old father of three who never attended church, asking for the hand in marriage of a twenty-year-old woman who had been raised with a strong Christian faith.

When he returned to New York City, Tom wrote to Lewis Miller asking for permission to marry his daughter. In his letter Tom wrote, "I trust you will not accuse me of egotism when I say that my life and history and standing are so well known as to call for no statement concerning myself. My reputation is so far made that I recognize I must be judged by it for good or ill." The response to Tom's letter was not enthusiastic, but the Millers did invite Tom to visit them in Akron, Ohio, before Christmas.

Nothing spurred Tom on like a challenge, and he set out to win over the Miller family. Mina's father turned out to be the easiest to convince. He and Tom had many things in common, and they spent many hours together discussing inventions and commerce. And Mina's two younger brothers, John and Theodore, liked Tom too, especially when he promised to send them equipment to make their own telegraph system. It was Mina's mother, Mary, and Mina's older sister Jenny who proved more difficult to win over. Both of them were worried about the age gap between Mina and Tom and the fact that Mina would be an instant mother to three children, with Dot being only seven years younger than Mina.

When Tom left Akron to return to New York City, he still did not have an answer as to whether the Miller clan would welcome him into their family. A few days after arriving home, he received his answer. Lewis and Mary Miller consented to the marriage of their daughter Mina to Thomas Edison.

Tom was elated and immediately turned his attention to providing a suitable new home for his bride-to-be. He looked at several huge estates before settling on Glenmont, an imposing mansion set on eleven acres of woodlands in West Orange, New Jersey. The house was set atop a knoll, and the New York City skyline could be seen in the distance.

Tom and Mina's wedding date was set for Wednesday, February 24, 1886, at the Miller home in Akron. As the day approached, Tom became nervous, especially since the planning was becoming more elaborate with each passing day. Tom, who was always self-conscious about his hearing when in a crowd, worried that he might not be able to follow the preacher and make the correct response when asked to say his vows.

Finally the day of the wedding arrived, and Tom, his brother Pitt, his sister Marion, and his father, Samuel, gathered in Akron for the ceremony. Once the Edison clan arrived at the Millers' mansion, Tom did his best to fulfill the expectations of his bride. He wore top hat and tails and stood tall as he waited for Mina to walk down the red carpet that led to the magnificent living room. Eighty people strained to catch a glimpse of Mina as she made her grand entrance on her father's arm. Tom thought she looked striking in her white silk gown. Mina was wearing the pearl necklace and diamond broach that he had given her as an engagement present.

The wedding went according to plan. Tom was able to hear the minister, and he recited his vows when asked, though he was relieved when it was all over and the orchestra struck up the wedding march.

At six o'clock that evening, the new Mr. and Mrs. Thomas Edison waited at the railway station to embark on the first leg of their long journey south to Fort Myers for their honeymoon. Tom had convinced Mina that Fort Myers was the ideal place for their honeymoon, and the trip would provide a good opportunity for him to check on the progress of his new house and laboratory.

The train ride from Akron to Fort Myers took a leisurely ten days, longer than first anticipated, but Tom and Mina were not concerned. Dot and the Gillilands had gone on ahead of them to Fort Myers to prepare the house. Unfortunately, things did not work out quite as planned. When Tom and Mina arrived in Fort Myers, they found that the new house was far from being finished. Even worse, they learned that the load of furnishings they had sent down before their wedding had been lost in a shipwreck.

Instead of staying in the new house, everyone moved into the Keystone Hotel and watched anxiously as work on the house progressed. A month after Tom and Mina's arrival in Fort Myers, the roof was finally put on the house, and everyone, including Mina's parents, who had come to visit, moved in. It was more like camping than anything else, but the weather was balmy, and Tom saw staying in the partially finished house as a grand adventure.

By the time April rolled around, everyone was ready to head back north. Tom looked forward to getting back to his work, but he was in for a shock when he arrived home.

"Strike! What do you mean the men are threatening to go on strike?" Tom asked, knowing perfectly well what the word meant.

"They have a list of demands, and they won't budge," Charles Batchelor replied. "The machine shop workers want to work only nine hours a day, not ten."

"And I suppose they want the same wages?" Tom grunted.

"They do, and double pay for overtime," Charles said.

"Think how far we would have got with that! I've worked twenty hours a day for weeks on end, and no one paid me overtime!" Tom snapped.

"They seem to think they want it. And they want to run only one machine each per shift. So we wouldn't be able to put one machinist on six lathes like we do now," Charles explained.

"Ridiculous! What's a man going to do, watch a lathe cut for two hours when he could be doing something else?"

Charles shrugged. "I'm just telling you what they want."

"Well they're not getting it. They can have the nine-hour day, but nothing else," Tom said firmly.

"I don't think it's going to be enough. They want a union to deal with these issues."

"I don't care. Let them strike if that's what they want to do. There'll never be a union in my factory," Tom snapped.

Strike is exactly what the men did. On May 17, 1886, 350 men walked out of the machine shop on Goerck Street, vowing not to return to work until their demands were met.

To make matters worse, things were getting off to a rocky start on the domestic front. Dot, who struggled with having a young, beautiful stepmother in the house, constantly started arguments with Mina and was quickly shipped off to attend boarding school. And although Mina had grown up in a wealthy home, she had not taken the time to observe the details of how the house was run. Now she was in charge of taking care of three children and running an enormous mansion with acres of grounds. She was overwhelmed by the task, and she soon hired a nanny for the boys, a cook, and several maids. Of course it took time and energy to supervise these workers.

Mina was soon feeling overworked and unhappy, and even more so when Tom reverted to his usual state in married life of seldom coming home for dinner. Tom even started sleeping at the factory some nights, which made Mina question how much he really loved her. Lack of love was not the problem. It was just that Tom's mind was so full of inventions and devices to improve that he seldom had the space or the time to think of anything else.

At the end of May the strike at the machine shop was still going strong, and it became clear to Tom that bigger issues were at stake. Tom's men were paid good money, up to forty dollars a week, but the cost of living was very high in New York City, and the manufacturing of power equipment there was spread among several small factories throughout the city. What Tom needed was one large factory complex outside the city where the men could build houses for their families and work away from the influence of New York union "communists," as Tom liked to call union organizers.

The new Edison United Manufacturing Company quickly took shape. Tom was able to buy ten acres of land in Schenectady, north of Albany, in upstate New York. The site had previously been owned by the McQueen Locomotive Works and already had two large brick buildings on it that could serve as manufacturing plants. It also had plenty of room to build more buildings. Work began immediately to equip the new facility to serve as a machine shop and manufacturing plant. As the new manufacturing facility was taking shape in Schenectady, Tom turned his attention back to an old invention that had been languishing—the phonograph. Tom's initial attempts to set up a company and market the phonograph had faltered several years before, but Tom had been much too preoccupied with developing the electric lightbulb and an electric supply system to do much about it. Others had not ignored the machine. Two inventors in Boston, Charles Tainter and Chichester Bell, Alexander Graham Bell's cousin, had worked at improving the phonograph. Rather than use the tinfoil Tom had used, they had added a cardboard cylinder covered with wax into which the needle carved a track. They had also greatly improved the mechanism that played back the recorded sound. They called their device a "graphophone," but because of Tom's patents, they had been unable to market the machine.

In 1885, however, Tom had failed to renew his British patent on the phonograph. According to the law of the day, when a foreign patent lapsed, so did the American patent. Tainter and Bell then patented their graphophone, with plans to produce and market it.

When Tom learned of this, he did not seem to mind. He was too busy with other things. But in October 1886 he again began to focus on the phonograph. He set up a laboratory at the Edison Lamp Works in East Newark, New Jersey, located about an hour from his Glenmont estate. There Tom began working on ways to improve the device. He built on the improvements that Tainter and Bell had made and looked for ways to power the phonograph with a small electric motor.

While at his lab at the Lamp Works, Tom also continued to conduct experiments to improve the filaments in his lightbulbs.

In December 1886, in the midst of trying to improve the phonograph, Tom caught a severe cold, which quickly progressed into pneumonia and pleurisy. Tom was confined to bed. In January 1887 Tom's manufacturing operations were officially transferred from New York City to Schenectady, and the new facility opened for business. Charles Batchelor was the plant's general manager, and John

Kruesi was supervisor and chief engineer. As the new plant opened, there was some doubt as to whether or not Tom would recover from his illness. Mina nursed her husband day and night, praying that he would not die.

Tom had a strong constitution, and eventually he began to recover. While he lay in bed at Glenmont recovering, he made a decision. He would build a new laboratory for himself nearby, and it would be grander than any other laboratory ever built.

When he was well enough to be up and about, Tom arranged to purchase a tract of land at the bottom of the knoll where Glenmont stood, on which he would build his new laboratory. Soon afterward he headed to Fort Myers to recuperate. While Tom was gone, Charles sketched out some rough plans for the new lab. When he returned to Glenmont from Florida, Tom hired an architect to draw up final plans for the building and oversee its construction.

The new laboratory building was to have three stories and be constructed of red brick. It would be 250 feet long, 50 feet wide, and 40 feet tall and provide 40,000 square feet of space. The building would also have an attached powerhouse. The first two floors of the structure were to be set up as a machine shop, and the third floor would provide space for conducting experiments. The entire western end of the building would be devoted to a two-and-a-half-story library.

Work soon began on the building, with Tom keeping a vigilant eye on things. As the construction progressed, Tom was not impressed with the quality of the workmanship he was seeing. He fired his architect, and Charles took over supervising the construction.

As work on the laboratory was nearing completion, Tom decided to add four more buildings to the site, each 100 feet long and 25 feet wide. These buildings were set parallel to each other and perpendicular to the main laboratory building. One building would be used for metallurgy, one for chemistry experiments, one for woodworking, and one for testing galvanometers. No iron was used in the construction of the galvanometer building, and copper nails were used to hold the building together so that no magnetic interference from metal would throw off the delicate instruments being tested in it.

When the new laboratory complex was complete, Tom had it stocked with every conceivable chemical, substance, and metal. He even ordered hog bristles, peacock feathers, porcupine quills, tanned walrus hides, bull's horns, elephant tusks, and all sorts of grains for the lab. The remaining chemicals and equipment from the now virtually abandoned Menlo Park laboratory were also transferred to the new facility.

On New Year's Day 1888 Tom was in a happy mood. He was feeling healthy again. His new laboratory complex was up and running, and he felt sure that it would be just as productive and profitable as the Menlo Park laboratory had been. Family life had settled down. The boys were doing well at home, Dot was off at boarding school, and Mina was expecting their first child around the end of May.

Chapter 13

Moving Pictures and Crushing Rocks

On May 31, 1888, Madeleine Edison was born. Tom and Mina were delighted to have another child. As 1888 progressed, Tom found himself busier than ever. His renewed interest in the phonograph led to the development of a better cylinder system for the device, which in turn involved applying for twenty-one separate patents.

The electric power system that Tom had developed was a direct-current system. As a result, the system was most efficient and economical at supplying electric current to an area of about one square mile around the generating station. This meant that to provide electricity to New York City with his system, he would need to establish thirty-six power-generating plants. Tom had discovered that this was not a cheap proposition. Despite the cost, he forged ahead, building more power stations in New York and laying cables under the streets. He also had built a generating plant in Chicago and was making plans to electrify that city as well.

As Tom's company kept busy installing new power-generating plants, the complaints from citizens began to grow. The people complained about the noise of the plants, the vibration they caused, and the thick, black smoke they belched into the air. People also complained about the constant flow of wagons through the streets bringing coal to the plants. And in Chicago, the workers in the Home Insurance Building, situated right next to Tom's generating plant, bemoaned the fact that their building constantly vibrated, creating an almost unbearable work environment.

Tom was undeterred. He was certain that such complaints would die down as people began to see and experience the benefits of electricity. But in 1888 Thomas Edison's direct-current system began to face competition from another system for generating power and delivering it to homes and buildings. The system was called alternating current (AC), and it was based on the principles worked out by one of Tom's former employees—Nikola Tesla—whose ideas Tom had dismissed as impractical.

In the spring of 1888 Tesla delivered a lecture titled *A New System of Alternating Current Motors and Transformers* to the American Institute of Electrical Engineers. One of those who heard the lecture was George Westinghouse, a Pittsburgh railroad entrepreneur who had decided to challenge Edison's seeming monopoly on providing electric power. Westinghouse engaged the services of Tesla as a consultant in his plan to set up an alternating-current electric supply system to compete with Tom.

Alternating current had the advantage of being able to be transformed. That is, the electric current could be stepped up to a higher voltage and later stepped down to a lower voltage, and Tesla had already developed the transformers needed to do this. What all of this meant was that alternating current generated at a power plant could then be transformed to a higher voltage and carried great distances over wires, where at the other end the voltage could be stepped down to a safe level for use in houses and buildings. As a result, an alternating current system would be cheaper to build and operate, since the power-generating plant would not have to be situated right in the heart of a city. And because it could be transformed, the current could be fed to a much greater area than the one square mile that Tom's plant could service.

Westinghouse, aided by Tesla, got to work establishing their alternating-current system. Other men and companies, persuaded by the theoretical advantages of AC power, also began to experiment with alternating-current systems.

Tom was unconvinced about the advantages of alternating current. Direct current, he declared, was a much safer current. To prove his point, he organized public demonstrations of just how unsafe alternating current was. He invited reporters and the public to the courtyard of his laboratory at West

Orange to watch as various animals were electro-cuted with alternating current. It was a grotesque display, but Tom was certain that it would lay to rest the matter of which electric current system was bet-ter. It did not. The advantages of alternating current were too great to ignore, and George Westinghouse and others forged ahead with their planned AC sys-tems. Soon some of those in Tom's own company were urging Tom to allow the development of an alternating-current system. Tom stubbornly refused.

In the spring of 1889, with an influx of capital from investors, Tom consolidated his business into an umbrella organization called the Edison General Electric Company. He also accepted a nomination to become a member of the New York Academy of Sciences. During 1889 Tom also allowed himself to be talked into planning a trip to Europe. He hated sailing and could not stand being away from his laboratory, but Mina convinced him to attend the Universal Exhibition being held in Paris in the fall of 1889 where the Edison Company was to have a huge display.

Mina left baby Madeleine with her mother, and she and Tom set sail for France. The voyage across the Atlantic Ocean was uneventful, and Tom spent many hours alone on deck staring at the surging waves. Other men might have dreamed of adven-tures or days gone by when pirates sailed the seas, but Thomas Edison dreamed of the future—of a time when the ocean itself would be harnessed to pro-vide all of the electrical power needs of the world.

When Tom and Mina finally arrived in Paris, they were astounded by the welcome they received. Tom's photo seemed to be plastered in the windows of every store and public building, and the city leaders proclaimed Tom "King." Of course none of this mattered much to Tom, but he did enjoy the social contacts his fame in Europe provided. During his stay he visited the most interesting men of the day in Paris. He toured Louis Pasteur's laboratory with him and lunched with Alexandre-Gustave Eiffel in his private salon atop the newly constructed Eiffel Tower, which at 300 meters tall was the tallest structure in the world and towered above the Universal Exhibition grounds. Tom also attended a dinner in honor of Louis Daguerre, who had developed early photography techniques. As well, the king of Italy sent an envoy to Paris to make Thomas Edison a grand officer of the Crown of Italy. Not to be outdone, the French made Tom Count Edison!

But the man who fascinated Tom the most was Etienne-Jules Marey, a French scientist who was working on the idea of photographing things as they moved. Marey did this using a "photographic gun," a simple camera with a revolving strip on which photographic plates were mounted, allowing the camera to record twelve photographs per second. When Tom visited him, Marey was using three cameras at a time to film the flight of a duck. By splicing together the pictures from the three cameras, Etienne-Jules Marey could record thirty-six photographs per second. When quickly flipped through, the overlapping images gave the impression of one continuous motion of the duck in flight. Tom was in fact looking at the first crude "movie," and the idea captivated him. He determined that once back in his laboratory in West Orange he would do something with the idea.

Tom and Mina arrived back at their Glenmont estate on October 6, 1889, after two exhausting months in Europe. Tom for one was glad to be home. His head was crammed with ideas for new projects and inventions. And once back in his laboratory, he decided to concentrate on the idea of developing a camera to record moving pictures. As he put it, he wanted to perfect "an instrument that does for the eye what the phonograph does for the ear."

As he started in on the project, Tom noted, "I had only one fact to guide me at all. This was the principle of optics technically called 'persistence of vision,' which proves that the sensation of light lingers in the brain for anywhere from one tenth to one one-hundredth of a second after the light itself has disappeared from sight of the eyes." This was the principle that caused a person to see the illusion of movement when the pages of a pad were flipped rapidly and the image on the page appeared to move. Tom's plan was to exploit this principle. He would devise a camera that could capture individual photos of an action at a fast rate. Thus, when the images were developed and run back at the same speed as they had been captured, the subject of the photos would appear to move, because the image of one photo would persist in the brain long enough for the next photo or frame to be moved into place and viewed.

As Tom saw it, the challenge was to produce a precisely timed mechanism that could move a photographic plate into place, capture an image on it, and move the next plate into place to capture the next image, all in a fraction of a second. This was a difficult mechanical challenge, one in which William Dickson, a member of Tom's experimental staff and also a photographer, aided Tom.

The task was simplified when George Eastman developed three-quarter-inch celluloid film, which could be rolled onto spools and fed through a camera. Tom saw its value to him in an instant. A length of celluloid film could be fed through the camera at a steady rate as it was rolled from one spool to another. As the film rolled past the back of the camera lens, images could be recorded on the film at a steady rate. The trick now was to develop both a transport mechanism to move the film through the camera at a constant pace and a shutter mechanism to open and close, also at a steady pace, to record images on the film.

Finally, after much experimenting, Tom and William came up with a mechanism that worked, capturing forty-six individual pictures of frames per second. Tom called his new camera a *kinetograph*, a name he derived from the Greek, meaning "moving writing."

The kinetograph was only half the equation. Tom could now capture moving images of film, but he needed a device to play those images back. He set to inventing the kinetoscope, from the Greek, meaning "moving view." The kinetoscope was a boxlike device. The developed film from the camera was wound on spools and placed inside the kinetoscope, which had an incandescent bulb set in the bottom of it. A person wanting to view the film looked through a peephole in the top of the device where a magnifying glass enlarged the image for the viewer. A clockwork motor twirled the spools, and as the film passed between the light and the magnifying glass, the person peering into the peephole was able to view the moving image.

At the same time that Tom was experimenting with moving images, he was focused on another venture—iron ore extraction. For years Tom had been interested in iron ore extraction and, in particular, using the power of magnetism to separate the ore. Nine years before, he had experimented with this process, using a magnet to separate iron from sand on the beaches of Massachusetts and Rhode Island. He decided it was now time to try his process on a larger scale.

With industrial growth in the United States came a great demand for steel. In the east of the country, however, many of the iron ore mines were becoming depleted. This was forcing steel-manufacturing plants to look farther afield for iron ore and, in the process, absorb the higher cost of transporting the ore to their plants. In truth iron ore was still left in the depleted mines. The trouble was, the amount of ore in the rocks was too low to be extracted by conventional methods. Tom believed that his process for extracting iron ore using magnetism could extract the iron from this low-grade ore.

Tom decided that the financial return on this venture would be great, and he wanted to corner the market for magnetic ore extraction. He began a campaign of buying up the mining rights of old or unproductive iron ore mines. At the same time, at an unproductive mine located three miles outside of Ogdensburg in northern New Jersey, he began constructing a huge plant to separate iron ore from the rock that contained it and concentrate that ore into briquettes that could be sold to steel-manufacturing plants.

The massive extraction plant consisted of sets of huge rollers through which huge chunks of rock were passed and eventually ground down to a fine powder so that a powerful magnet could extract the tiny particles of iron ore from the powder.

Setting up the plant kept Tom busy for months. In the midst of Tom's busy schedule, on August 3, 1890, Mina gave birth to her second child, and a third son for Tom. They named the baby Charles, after Tom's nephew Charley. Tom hoped that the boy would grow up to be just as mechanically inclined as his namesake. Tom's older three children, however, were not amounting to much in Tom's eyes. Dot was in Europe with Mina's two younger sisters and a chaperone, and she seemed to have no idea about money, constantly writing home asking her father to send more money. The two boys, Tom Jr. and Will, were now away at boarding school, but they sent a stream of letters home complaining about how sick they felt and making excuses for their poor grades. Tom had little to do with them, leaving Mina to remind his children of their duty to live up to the family name.

The year 1891 did not begin well for Tom. In January he received word that his older brother Pitt had died broken and penniless at the age of fifty-nine. Tom did not want to attend the funeral, but his sister Marion pressured him into returning to Port Huron, Michigan, for the service.

When he returned from Port Huron, Tom sold some of his stock and paid off the mortgage on Glenmont. Then he signed the place over to his wife. Whatever happened in his business dealings, he did not want to end up homeless and penniless as had his brother, and he trusted Mina to watch over the home finances.

Meanwhile, Tom was experiencing trouble with his iron ore extraction operation. Although the process was working well, the problem was that the quality of the ore he was getting was not as high as Tom hoped, and so the plant was running at a loss. Yet Tom remained upbeat about the endeavor. He was certain that given enough time he would overcome these difficulties, and he spent much of his time throughout the rest of the year at the Ogdensburg facility.

In 1891, the board of directors of Edison General Electric tried to force Tom to produce an alternating-current power system, but Tom stubbornly balked at the suggestion. The matter finally came to a head in February 1892. The major investors in the company became so frustrated with Tom's refusal that they proposed a merger of Edison General Electric with the Thomson-Houston Company, a competitor in the lighting and electric business, and a company that was developing an alternating-current system. The board of directors approved the merger, and a new company was formed that would be called General Electric. Tom did not approve of the merger, but since he did not hold a controlling interest in Edison General Electric, he could do little about it. He was made a director in the new company, though he rarely attended board meetings, choosing instead to focus on his other interests.

One of those other interests was motion pictures. Now that he had invented the kinetograph and the kinetoscope, in December 1892 Tom embarked on another project associated with these devices, the building of the Black Maria—the first ever motion picture studio. The Black Maria was basically a tar-paper shack built on the grounds of Tom's West Orange laboratory. Tom would later describe the place saying,

> Our studio was almost as amazing as the pictures we made in it. We were looking for service, not art. The building was about twenty-five by thirty feet in dimensions, and we gave a grotesque effect to the roof by slanting it up in a hunch in the center and arranging shutters that could be opened or

closed with a pulley to obtain the greatest benefit from the light. Then, in order to make certain of as long a day as possible, we swung the whole building on pivots, like an old-fashioned river bridge, so it could be turned to follow the course of the sun. We covered it with tar paper, and painted it a dead black inside to bring our actors into sharp relief. It was a ghastly proposition for a stranger daring enough to brave its mysteries—especially when it began to turn like a ship in a gale. But we managed to make pictures there. And, after all, that was the real test.

The Black Maria was finished in May 1893, just as an economic recession hit the country. As a result of the poor economic times, Tom was forced to lay off many workers, some of whom had been with him for a number of years, and suspend many activities at his laboratory. Despite the uncertain time, Tom forged ahead with his iron ore business, selling off large blocks of his shares in General Electric in order to keep the operation afloat financially.

Tom was able to survive the economic depression, but he had to work harder than ever to stay ahead of disaster. He spent most of his week at the iron ore plant in northern New Jersey, seeing his family only on weekends.

Mina adjusted to looking after the family and managing the estate without any input from Tom. She also busied herself in a variety of activities. On

Mondays she held a luncheon for the neighborhood women. On Tuesdays she hosted dancing classes for Madeleine and her friends. Wednesdays were devoted to art at the Orange Women's Club, and Thursdays, to music concerts at the country club. Then on Fridays Mina hosted another women's luncheon. Every night she wrote a letter home to her family, outlining the activities of the day. Even though they were many miles away in Ohio, her family knew a lot more about her and the children's daily activities than Tom did.

During August and September of 1893, Tom did take time off to travel to Chicago with Mina and members of her family to attend the World's Columbian Exposition, which was being held to celebrate the four-hundredth anniversary of Christopher Columbus's discovery of America. It was a fantastic affair, and of course many of Tom's achievements were on display in the Manufacturing and Liberal Arts Building and in Electricity Hall. In fact, shooting up in the middle of Electricity Hall was the Edison Tower of Light, an eighty-foot-high replica of an electric lightbulb covered with thousands of tiny prisms and surrounded by strings of lightbulbs that blinked on and off. Even Tom had to admit that it was quite a spectacle.

In January 1894 William Dickson, Tom's associate who helped in developing the kinetograph and the kinetoscope, produced the first motion picture to receive a copyright. The short film, shot in the Black Maria studio, was titled *Edison Kinetographic Record of a Sneeze*. And that is exactly what it was—

a film showing Fred Ott, one of Tom's workers, sneez-ing. It may not have seemed like much, but a new era of entertainment had begun. William Dickson made and copyrighted seventy-five more films throughout 1894.

Reflecting on the future of motion pictures, Tom wrote:

> I consider that the greatest mission of the motion picture is first to make people happy... to bring more joy and cheer and wholesome good will into this world of ours. And God knows we need it.

> Second—to educate, elevate, and inspire. I believe that the motion picture is destined to revolutionize our educational system, and that in a few years it will supplant largely, if not entirely, the use of text-books in our schools. Books are clumsy methods of instruction at best, and often even the words of explanation in them have to be explained.

> I should say that on average we get only about two percent efficiency out of school books as they are written to-day. The educa-tion of the future, as I see it, will be conducted through the medium of the motion picture, a visualized education, where it should be possi-ble to obtain a one-hundred percent efficiency.

> The motion picture has tremendous possi-bilities for the training and development of the memory. There is no medium for memory-building as productive as the human eye.

That is another basic reason for the motion picture in the school. It will make a more alert and more capable generation of citizens and parents. You can't make a trained animal unless you start with a puppy. It is next to impossible to teach an old dog new tricks.

I do not believe that any other single agency of progress has the possibilities for a great and permanent good to humanity that I can see in the motion picture. And those possibilities are only beginning to be touched.

While Tom had big dreams for motion pictures, by 1895 his dream of dominating the iron ore industry in the United States was floundering. He had spent over one million dollars of his own money on the project, but no matter how hard he tried, he just could not seem to make the business profitable. And this situation was not helped by a decline in the price of iron ore during the recession of 1893. Still, Tom remained optimistic. Somehow, he believed, he could still make the whole business work profitably.

Chapter 14

"Yes, sir, it's mostly hard work."

A stonishing. Now here's a mystery I can get my hands on!" Tom exclaimed as he read the *New York Times* one morning early in February 1896. As usual he was not talking to anyone in particular, just himself. The article he was reading was about Wilhelm Conrad Roentgen, a physics professor at Würzburg University in Germany, who had noticed a strange phenomenon while performing an experiment. On November 8, 1895, the professor was experimenting with a Crookes tube (a glass bulb with a partial vacuum inside that was used for studying high-tension voltage discharges called cathode rays) when he noticed that if the tube was enclosed in a sealed, thick black carton to exclude all light in a dark room, and a paper plate covered on one side with barium-platinocyanide was placed up to two meters from the tube, the tube would glow.

During further experiments to investigate this phenomenon, Roentgen discovered that objects of different thicknesses placed in the path of the rays from the Crookes tube had a variable amount of transparency to them when the image of the object was recorded on a photographic plate. The professor then placed his wife's hand over a photographic plate and in the path of the rays from the tube for several minutes. When he developed the plate, he discovered an image of her hand that showed the shadows thrown by the bones of her hand and by a ring she was wearing. The shadows were surrounded by a lighter outline of the flesh, which was more permeable to the rays coming from the tube and so threw a fainter shadow.

Roentgen knew that the image he was seeing could not have been cast by the cathode rays (or electron beams) that the Crookes tube was designed to emit. Such rays could not penetrate air for any significant distance. The images had been cast by some other kind of rays, and since the professor did not know what they were, he named them X-rays, the "X" indicating that the rays were unknown.

Tom loved a puzzle—and a competition—and after reading the article in the newspaper, he decided that with x-rays he had both. Someone was going to find a way to use Professor Roentgen's experiments and produce a clearer x-ray image, and Tom decided to be that someone.

The first thing Tom set out to improve was the quality of the Crookes tube. He made its exterior walls thinner, and increased power to the electrodes inside the tube. Then he tried over two thousand chemicals inside the tube to see which one would produce x-rays that gave a clearer image on a photographic plate. Tom was so absorbed in this work that when he received word that his ninety-two-year-old father had died on February 26, 1896, he did not plan to attend the funeral. As she had done when their brother Pitt died, Tom's older sister Marion put pressure on Tom. So Tom made the journey to Ohio, where the funeral was held, and then on to Port Huron, where his father's body was laid to rest in a grave next to his mother's grave. Throughout the journey and the funeral, however, Tom's mind was never far from thoughts of improving x-ray images.

By the time Tom got back to Glenmont, a pile of letters was awaiting him from people who had heard about his experiments with x-rays. One man, who had been eating glass and metal objects since he was a child, wanted an x-ray to see what had happened to the things he had eaten. Another man wanted to buy a pair of x-ray goggles so that he could read the back of playing cards, and a millionaire wanted to see an x-ray image of his brain. X-rays had ignited the imagination of the public and Tom's as well. Tom saw many practical applications for the new technology, including x-raying teeth to find cavities and using x-ray to treat acne.

Within weeks of returning to his laboratory after his father's funeral, Tom discovered a chemical compound that left a bright x-ray image. The substance was calcium tungstate. Tom wrote to Lord Kelvin, the famous British physicist, and reported his discovery to him. Unlike his other inventions and discoveries, Tom never tried to patent this discovery. He wanted the improved x-rays to be put to use as soon as possible so that images made from them could be used to help in diagnosing people's illnesses.

Tom continued to do his own medical experiments with x-rays. He took hundreds of x-ray pictures of two volunteers, brothers Charles and Clarence Dally. After a month of experimenting, the brothers noticed that their skin looked as though it had been burned. They also reported to Tom that they were suffering from headaches and nausea. Tom was mortified. He had noticed the same things happening to him, and *he* normally stood *behind* the x-ray apparatus, not in front of it, while making images.

It was not long before Clarence became very ill. He developed cancerous lesions on his hands, and eventually his doctor was forced to amputate both his arms. Cancer also broke out on Clarence's face, and the doctor could do nothing but wait for Clarence to die. At the same time Tom noticed lumpy growths protruding from his own abdomen, and he decided to stop all further experiments with x-rays. He felt guilty that Clarence Dally was dying, and given the growths in his stomach, he wondered whether his own death might not be far behind.

Thomas Edison still had a lot of life left in him, however. With his x-ray experiments behind him, Tom looked around for a new challenge.

Toward the end of the 1890s, automobiles were beginning to make their appearance in America. They were ungainly looking contraptions powered by either steam, an internal combustion engine, or electric power. Tom, who did not like horses, took an immediate interest in motorcars and, in particular, those that were powered by electric motors. He disliked the internal combustion engine, thinking it inefficient and dirty. But as he studied electric-powered cars more closely, Tom soon saw their weakness. These cars derived their power from lead-sulphur batteries that were heavy, did not last long, and were prone to corrosion. If electric cars were to become commercially viable, Tom reasoned, they needed a better battery. So Tom began thinking about developing such a battery.

In the meantime, Tom's family was growing up. The year before, in 1895, much to Tom and Mina's chagrin, Dot had married a German army officer. Now she wanted her father to send enough money to support both her and her husband. Her new mother-in-law had even written to Tom suggesting that he was being stingy and that his daughter deserved better treatment. Such an accusation made Tom furious. Tom had started earning his keep when he was only twelve years old and had worked hard all his life, yet none of his three oldest children appeared to have any idea about how to earn a living. Tom Jr. drank away most of the money he was given, and Will was fanatical about motorcars.

What a contrast Tom Jr. and Will were to Mina's two younger brothers. The boys were all about the same age, but John and Theodore Miller were accomplished scholars. Theo played the piano beautifully, and both boys took full responsibility for their futures. In April 1898, when President McKinley declared that the United States was at war with Spain, Theodore and then John signed up to fight right away. Theo, who had been studying law in New York City, joined Theodore Roosevelt's Rough Riders. Will Edison finally got around to joining the navy just three days before the Spanish-American War ended.

Mina and Tom hosted a farewell for Mina's brothers at Glenmont. Mina was pregnant with her and Tom's third child, but she insisted on staging a grand sendoff for her favorite brothers.

Three months later, on July 10, 1898, Mina gave birth to another son. While she and Tom were deciding what to name their new son, they received a telegram from Cuba conveying the tragic news that Theodore Miller had died from wounds he sustained at the Battle of San Juan Hill ten days before. The new baby was immediately named Theodore Miller Edison, after Mina's dead brother. Tom, who never knew what to do around grieving people, quickly retreated to his laboratory.

Within five months of Theodore's death, Mina's older sister and her father also died, and Tom received a shock of his own. Tom Jr. announced that he had secretly married an actress named Marie Louise Toohey. Marie Toohey had a reputation for being an opportunist, and by the time Tom learned of the marriage, Tom Jr. was already plotting a divorce from his new wife.

It was a grim time for the Edison family, as well as for Tom's business dealings. Near the end of 1898 a huge supply of high-grade iron ore was discovered in northern Minnesota. Its discovery was the last straw for Tom's iron ore extraction business, and Tom declared the venture over. He had spent over one and a half million dollars on the project, and its demise left him near broke. Still, Tom could not bring himself to worry about the past. "The money's all gone," he announced to his assistant Walter Mallory, "but we had a heck of a good time spending it, didn't we?"

The time Tom had spent refining his iron ore crushing and extraction machinery was not a total loss. Tom moved the machinery to eastern Pennsylvania to use it to crush limestone to a powder to make cement. The huge machines did a better job at crushing the limestone than did his competitors' machines. This, in addition to the larger kiln Tom developed to bake the powder, meant that he was soon producing the highest-quality cement available in the United States. On June 7, 1899, Tom incorporated the Edison Portland Cement Company.

In the fall of 1899 Will Edison married Blanche Travers in another marriage that displeased Tom. Now all three of Tom and Mary's children were married, and in Tom's opinion, all of them had made poor choices for spouses.

In May 1901 a crisis of another sort gripped the Edison household. A message stamped on brown paper arrived at the door. It read, "If you dont put $25,000 gold for next Thursday night at 12,30 at foot of sign Hahne & Co. in Central & Essex Avenues Orange N.J. We will kidnap your child if you notify the Police We shall do you same."

Upon receiving the threat, Tom not only went to the police but also hired his own private eye and a bodyguard for the family. The kidnapping never took place, but Tom kept the private eye, mainly to follow up on the antics of his sons Tom Jr. and Will.

Thomas Alva Edison Jr. presented the most problems. Sharing the name of his now-famous father proved too much of a temptation. Soon after his marriage to Marie Toohey fell apart, Tom Jr. had become a street bum in New York City, where he was "found" by a hustler, and the two men had gone into business together. The Edison name was golden, and Tom Jr. had soon lent his name to the Edison Jr. Electric Light and Power Company and to the Thomas A. Edison Jr. Chemical Company, which manufactured "Wizard Ink Tablets" and the "Magno Electric Vitalizer."

Many of the products the two companies sold were scams, and the private eye was soon reporting to Tom that his son was passing bad checks, drinking heavily, and being investigated for mail fraud. In the face of these problems, Tom Jr. turned to his uncle, Charles Stilwell, for advice. His uncle slyly suggested that they should both approach Tom for money in exchange for Tom Jr.'s changing his name.

By now Tom was not surprised by the antics of his son, and he signed a contract with him. In exchange for Tom's paying Tom Jr. thirty-five dollars a week and Charles Stilwell twenty-five dollars, Thomas Alva Edison Jr. pledged to change his name and not to enter into any business without Tom's express approval.

The situation with his family was a bitter blow to Tom, but he had a lot of new ideas, and as usual he buried himself in his work.

With the iron ore extraction business no longer pressing on his time, Tom felt free to pursue developing a better battery. The process of developing a better battery than the lead-sulphur batteries currently in use turned out to be a demanding process. Tom and his associates at the laboratory conducted thousands of experiments testing various chemicals and metals for their electrical characteristics. Eventually all the experimental work paid off, and Tom produced an iron-nickel battery that used an alkaline electrolyte made from potash, rather than the sulfuric acid that proved so corrosive in the old lead-sulphur batteries. And his new battery was a third lighter, lasted longer, and charged more quickly than the old batteries.

Satisfied with his invention, in early 1903 Tom set up a factory to mass-produce the new batteries at Silver Lake in nearby Bloomfield, New Jersey. Soon 450 men were busy turning out iron-nickel batteries, and eager customers were waiting to snap them up.

Once again Tom's hard work had paid off, though developing the battery had proved to be a much greater task than he had first imagined. When a new employee congratulated him on his luck with the battery, Tom retorted,

I do not believe in luck at all. And if there is such a thing as luck, then I must be the most unlucky fellow in the world. I've never once made a lucky strike in all my life. When I get after something that I need, I start finding everything in the world that I don't need—one...thing after another. I find ninety-nine things that I don't need, and then comes number one hundred, and that—at the very last—turns out to be just what I had been looking for. It's got to be so that if I find something in a hurry, I git to doubting whether it's the real thing; so I go over it carefully and it generally turns out to be wrong.... Most fellows try a few things and then quit. I never quit until I git what I'm after.... Then again, a lot of people think that I have done things because of some "genius" that I've got. That too is not true. Any other bright-minded fellow can accomplish just as much if he will stick [to it] and remember that nothing that's any good works by itself, just to please you; you got to make the...thing work. You may have heard people repeat what I have said "Genius is one percent inspiration, ninety-nine percent perspiration." Yes, sir, it's mostly hard work.

Tom's new batteries had their problems. The potash solution inside the batteries slowly ate away at the solder holding the cases together, and the batteries began to leak. They also were prone to short circuits, and they lost power after only three or four months' use. As problems with the new batteries mounted, Tom decided in November 1904 to pull them from the market and close down the factory, at least until he had discovered why they behaved so erratically and he could correct the problem.

Finding the problem and correcting it took longer than Tom could have imagined. It was not until July 1909 that production began of a redesigned cobalt-nickel alkaline battery. The new battery was a masterpiece of electrochemical engineering. Once again eager customers were snapping up the new batteries, which sold for several hundred dollars each. The new batteries, however, were not well suited for the purpose for which they had been designed—providing power to run electric cars. While the new battery was powerful and held its charge well, it was larger than existing batteries and produced only 1.1 volts per cell as opposed to the 1.95 volts per cell that a lead-sulphuric acid battery produced. This meant that more than one battery would have to be installed in a vehicle, negating the weight advantage Tom had strived for.

To make matters worse, the internal combustion engine had supplanted electricity as the motive power for motorcars and trucks. Henry Ford, who had once worked as chief engineer at the Detroit Edison Company's power-generating plant, had perfected a cheap 15-horsepower, 4-cylinder internal combustion engine. The engine was installed in the new Model T car that Ford had introduced the year before. His vehicle was fast becoming the car of choice for the masses in the United States.

Nonetheless, Tom's cobalt-nickel alkaline battery was a good battery, and it was soon being put to work for a number of other purposes. Mine owners used it in their coal mines to provide light for their workers, and railroad companies used it to power their signals. It was even put to work powering submarines for the U.S., Russian, and Argentine navies.

With the development of the cobalt-nickel alkaline battery finally behind him, in 1910 Tom returned to improving the phonograph. This was a bittersweet moment for him, though, as Charles Batchelor, his longtime associate who had been by Tom's side as he invented the phonograph, had died that year on January 1.

In the intervening years others had tinkered at improving the phonograph, most notably Emile Berliner, who had developed a commercial disc phonograph. Disc records were longer playing and easier to store. Despite these advantages, Tom had held firm to his belief that cylinder recordings produced superior sound. However, by 1907 sales of disc phonographs had surpassed those of Tom's cylinder phonograph. Tom was forced to concede the point, and he set to work developing a disc phonograph of his own. In particular he focused on developing a higher-quality record surface and on recording and reproducing music with greater fidelity.

Tom succeeded in his efforts: his disc phonograph and records were technically superior. However, they were also incompatible with the machines of his competitors. As well Tom failed to adapt to the demand for popular singers. He insisted that only those artists whose voices he personally considered superior be recorded and sold on records for his new phonograph. As a result, despite the technical excellence of Tom's improvements to the phonograph, sales of the device, while good, never returned to their previous level.

In 1912 Henry Ford came to the West Orange laboratory to meet with Tom. Tom had briefly met Ford in 1896 soon after Ford had built his first car, the quadricycle, though Tom said he could not recall the meeting. Now Ford was producing a quarter of all the motorcars sold in the United States, and he and Tom soon struck up a deep friendship.

Ford's Model T car, like virtually every internal combustion car of the day, derived its power from a magneto that sparked to life once the car was started. This meant that the car had to be cranked by hand to start. To improve on the popularity of his car and to make it a more acceptable vehicle for women to drive, Ford wanted to equip the Model T with an automatic starting system. For this, he explained to Tom, he needed to have designed a battery, a starter motor, and a generator to recharge the battery as the car was running. He asked Tom to create these items for him and advanced him one hundred thousand dollars to begin work immediately.

Tom threw himself into the task, and as usual he expected all those around him to be equally enthusiastic. He worked 112 hours a week at the laboratory and set goals that no one could reach. One night, for instance, he suggested to one of his young assistants that the two of them work on a particular problem together and make a joint resolution not to sleep until they had solved it. The young assistant was horrified. "Mr. Edison, you know I have been at the problem for months. I have tried every reasonable thing I could think of, and no result. Not even a lead!"

"That's just where your trouble has been," Tom chuckled. "You have tried only reasonable things. Reasonable things never work. Since you can't think up any more reasonable things, you'll have to begin thinking up *un*reasonable things to try, and then you'll hit the solution in no time. After that, you can take a nap."

In fact the solution to the problem took several more weeks to discover.

Tom was now sixty-five years old, and although he worked eighteen hours a day, he also saw the need to take vacations away from all the demands of inventing. One wonderful opportunity to do this came when he was staying at his winter home in Fort Myers, Florida. Henry Ford drove down to visit Tom, bringing along with him the elderly and famous naturalist John Burroughs. The three men were all very different, but they all needed a break. They decided to go off for a jaunt through the Everglades. The trip was so successful that the three of them agreed to make it an annual event, with Tom nominated to choose the route of each new motoring adventure.

Back at Glenmont, Mina was trying to guide her three children into successful careers and marriages, but Madeleine, Charles, and Theodore proved just as stubborn as their three older half-siblings. At twenty-three years of age, Madeleine announced that she was unofficially engaged to John Sloane, the son of a prominent Catholic doctor. This was too much for the staunchly Protestant Mina, who stalled the marriage, hoping that Madeleine would change her mind. But Madeleine did not, and the couple were married in June 1914, when Madeleine was twenty-six.

Six months later, Tom had quite a different situation on his hands. On the night of December 9, 1914, the phone rang at Glenmont. Fire had broken out in the film-inspection booth and was spreading rapidly through the old wooden buildings that made up the Edison laboratory and manufacturing complex in West Orange. Tom rushed out the door, with his son Charles behind him. Charles, who often acted as chauffeur for his father, since Tom refused to drive any vehicle, got behind the wheel of the family's car, and the two of them charged down the hill to the laboratory.

Tom and Charles arrived at the laboratory at the same time as the puny Orange Fire Department. Together they soon discovered that there was not enough water at the site to fight the flames. Already huge plumes of multicolored smoke rose above the burning buildings as a cocktail of chemicals, oils, celluloid, and wax ignited. Tom and Charles joined the laboratory workers, who were dragging flammable materials away from nearby buildings in the hope that those buildings would be spared from the flames.

Two hours passed, and Tom retreated to the storage-battery building to watch helplessly as the flames grew bigger. By now six buildings were engulfed in flames, and although fire departments from Newark and other communities had arrived, they could do little to fight the blaze without a steady supply of water. Instead they concentrated their efforts on trying to keep the main laboratory buildings from catching on fire. The fire could be seen for miles. Crowds gathered to watch the pyrotechnic display, and it was 11:00 PM before the flames finally died out.

By the time the fire was over, Tom was exhausted. He had just endured some of the worst hours of his life, but already he was looking on the bright side of things and was planning for the future. He scribbled a note and handed it to a nearby reporter. The note read, "Am pretty well burned out but tomorrow there will be some rapid mobilizing when I find out where I am at. Although I am sixty-seven years old, I will start all over again tomorrow. I will begin to clear out the debris if [it is] cool enough, and I will go right back to work rebuilding the plant."

Chapter 15

Benefactor of Mankind

Damage to Tom's laboratory and manufacturing complex in West Orange was estimated to be between three million and five million dollars. But true to his word, the next day Tom and his workers set to work cleaning up the mess. Although the fire burned the phonograph production building, the manufacturing equipment inside was not damaged. It was moved to the storage-battery facility, and within a month production of phonographs and disks was back up and running. Wagonloads of debris were carted away from the site, and rebuilding of the destroyed buildings soon began.

The future looked bright again, except for the war that had engulfed Europe. Britain and France and their allies were locked in a bloody fight against Germany, the Austro-Hungarian Empire, and the

Ottoman Empire. But as awful as reports of the fighting were in the newspapers, most people, including Tom, agreed that the war was not America's problem, that is until May 7, 1915. On that date the passenger liner RMS *Lusitania*, on its way from New York to Great Britain and carrying 128 Americans, was torpedoed and sunk by a German U-boat off the coast of Ireland. Public opinion in the United States changed as a result, and most people believed it would be only a matter of time before the country was drawn into the war in Europe.

Two weeks after the sinking of the *Lusitania*, Secretary of the Navy Josephus Daniels paid Tom a visit at his West Orange laboratory and ordered fifteen million dollars' worth of batteries for American battleships and submarines. Tom talked with the secretary for a long time, and he obviously made a great impression. Two months later Secretary Daniels proposed that the United States Navy form a "department of invention and development" to come up with ideas to improve and design military inventions. And so in the fall of 1915, the Naval Consulting Board was established, with Thomas Edison as the board's chairman.

Tom plunged right into the challenge. He gave responsibility of the laboratory and the day-to-day running of his various manufacturing plants to his son Charles and moved to a hotel in Washington, D.C., to be near Navy headquarters. It was nearly two more years before the United States entered the war in 1917. By that time Tom and his team of inventors had come up with some very useful ideas.

Among these were modified periscopes for submarines with rotating spray-free viewfinders,
improved torpedoes, a rapid-shutter Venetian-blind
searchlight that could be used by warships to signal
each other in code at up to forty words per minute,
an antirust coating for submarine guns, a light-
weight silicate of soda fire extinguisher, a hydrogen
gas detector for submarines to avoid explosions, and
improved accuracy of ships' guns.

The list of achievements was impressive, yet
despite them, Tom soon found that the United States
Navy ran at a much more measured pace than a
private laboratory. Ideas could not be put into prac-
tice without hundreds of trials and signatures of
approval. All of this took a great deal of time, and in
fact World War I was over in 1918 before many of
the Naval Consulting Board's recommendations
could be put to good use.

The post–World War I years brought many technological changes, one of which was the advent of
radio. Initially Tom dismissed the radio as a fad and
refused to believe Charles when he insisted that it
would one day become even more popular than the
phonograph.

Tom should have listened to his son. In 1922
Americans bought sixty million dollars' worth of
radios, and in 1926 they spent over five hundred
million dollars on them. It was not long before one
in every three homes in the United States owned a
radio receiver. Thomas Edison had overlooked a
wonderful opportunity. But by then he was an old
man of seventy-five, and it was hard for him to keep

up with new trends. So much had changed in his lifetime. Men and women flew in airplanes, drove around in motorcars, talked with each other on the telephone, went to the movies, and listened to the radio and to music on the phonograph. Tom had had a hand in inventing or improving many of these things that people now took for granted in their everyday lives.

In 1926 Tom retired as the president of Thomas Alva Edison Inc., the company under which he had gathered together all his various manufacturing operations. As expected, his son Charles took his place as president, while Tom remained chairman of the board.

Mina had big plans for Tom now that he was no longer involved with his business on a day-to-day basis. She arranged a round of social visits and expected her husband to arrive at the dinner table in full formal dress. A parade of the world's famous people were soon making their way to Glenmont to visit with the Edisons. Among them were the King and Queen of Siam, Herbert Hoover, Orville Wright, Charles and Anne Lindbergh, and Helen Keller. More often than not, Tom could not follow the conversation. His hearing had been deteriorating over the years. Mina would sit beside him and patiently tap out the words in Morse code on his hand. Sometimes Tom fell asleep at the table and had to be nudged awake between the main course and dessert.

Tom, for his part, did not care whether or not people came to visit him, unless they wanted to talk about the latest inventions and discoveries of the day. Then he had a thousand questions to ask them.

Although he was officially retired, Tom never stopped thinking up new ideas. His old friend Henry Ford was producing more cars a month than ever, and there was a fast-growing demand for rubber to make tires. Tom decided to see if he could find a plant native to the American continent that could be used to produce rubber. On his eightieth birthday, in February 1927, he announced the founding of his new company, the Edison Botanic Research Corporation, to investigate new forms of rubber. Once again, Tom had a mission. He set out every Sunday afternoon with his driver to look for new plant specimens to test. He also hired field men to send him plant samples from all over the country. When that did not yield the results he wanted, he sent his men farther afield to Canada and South America in search of suitable plants.

In the fall of 1928, Tom reluctantly took time out to receive the Congressional Gold Medal. The official ceremony was held at West Orange, with a radio hookup to the White House so that President Calvin Coolidge could participate. In his speech for the occasion, the president declared,

Noble, kindly servant of the United States and benefactor of mankind, may you long be spared to continue your work and to inspire those who will carry forward your torch. Few men have possessed to such a striking degree the blending of the imagination of a dreamer with the practical, driving force of a doer.... Although Edison belongs to the world, the United States takes pride in the thought that his rise from humble beginnings and his unceasing struggle to overcome the obstacles on the road to success illustrate the spirit of our country.

Henry Ford agreed with the president's sentiments. He was developing a museum, to be called Greenfield Village, in Dearborn, Michigan. He decided to open it in conjunction with the golden jubilee, or fiftieth anniversary, of Tom's breakthrough with the incandescent lightbulb. The date was set for October 21, 1929. And what better way to honor Tom's great achievements, Henry Ford decided, than to have Tom's Menlo Park laboratory constructed on the site so that those who came to Greenfield Village could experience for themselves the surroundings in which some of the greatest inventions in history were made.

Ford's workers went to Menlo Park, where they carefully deconstructed what was left of Tom's old laboratory. They had the remains of the building transported to Dearborn, where the lab was rebuilt and restored on the grounds of Greenfield Village. Meanwhile Ford scoured the country for the original equipment that Tom and his team had used in the laboratory. He even hired Francis Jehl, Tom's first assistant, to come to Dearborn and oversee the meticulous reconstruction of Menlo Park.

Greenfield Village was also designed to showcase the work of many other inventors. Wilbur and Orville Wright's bicycle shop was reconstructed on the site, and reproductions of other famous buildings, including Independence Hall in Philadelphia, were added.

Altogether, Henry Ford amassed two million dollars' worth of artifacts for his new venture, making it the largest "living" museum of its kind in the world.

Finally everything was ready, and on October 21, 1929, an old wood-burning train, just like the one Tom had worked on as a boy, transported Tom, Mina, Henry and Clara Ford, and President and Mrs. Herbert Hoover from Detroit to Greenfield Village. Tom could not resist grabbing a basketful of fruit and walking up and down the aisle pretending to hawk goods to the passengers, as he had done as a candy butch seventy years before. It was the first of hundreds of memories Tom would relive that day.

At Dearborn a host of important people waited to meet the train. Amid the crowd were old friends and new faces including Marie Curie, George Eastman, Will Rogers, John D. Rockefeller, and Charles Schwab. The day was filled with feasting, speech-making, and inspecting Greenfield Village. The highlight of the day was a reenactment of the lighting of the first successful incandescent lightbulb.

It felt eerie to Tom to be back in his old Menlo Park laboratory, especially since the lab had been in ruins the last time he drove by the place. At one point in the proceedings Henry Ford took Tom aside and asked, "So what do you think of the lab?"

"It's ninety-nine and one-half percent perfect," Tom retorted.

Ford's face fell. "What's the matter with the other half percent?" Ford asked.

"We never kept it as clean as this!" Tom chuckled.

At the end of the day Tom was exhausted from socializing with old friends and new, especially since he was the center of attention. By the end of the event, he could hardly wait to go to Fort Myers, Florida, for the winter months. Awaiting him at Fort Myers were five freight cars of goldenrod plants, which Tom felt certain could be processed into high-quality rubber.

Although he still got up and worked on various projects each morning, Tom realized that he was slowing down. He was not well a lot of the time, and his doctor told him that he was suffering from kidney disease and diabetes. Tom decided to treat the ailments himself by going on a diet of milk only, supplemented with an occasional glass of orange juice.

For his eighty-third birthday Mina gave him a wheelchair, and Tom agreed to be wheeled around the estate grounds each afternoon. Tom's children came to visit him at Glenmont, and Tom had finally slowed down enough to welcome their company.

Marion (Dot) had divorced her German husband and now lived quietly in Connecticut. Tom Jr. had resumed using his own name, was remarried, and now lived on a mushroom farm. Will and his wife Blanche ran a chicken farm.

Of all his children, Madeleine, whose husband, John Sloane, worked for an airplane manufacturing business, was the only Edison child to produce grandchildren—four grandsons, Thomas, John, Peter, and Michael.

Meanwhile Charles Edison continued to serve as the president of Thomas Alva Edison Inc. Theodore helped Charles out where he could, though his heart was in preserving the natural environment. Both sons were now married but remained childless.

Tom continued planning and experimenting into his eighty-fourth year, but his journals began to be increasingly full of the things he hoped to do soon, rather than a record of what he was currently doing.

In early September 1931, Tom's kidneys began to fail. The information was leaked to the press, and reporters set up a round-the-clock vigil to monitor Tom's last days. The eyes of the world were on Glenmont. President and Mrs. Hoover sent Tom flowers, the pope sent him a personal message, and thousands of get-well cards arrived from all over the world.

An oxygen tank was installed in Tom's bedroom to help him breathe, but in his usual stubborn way, Tom refused to use it. Tom's world continued to narrow, until on Sunday, October 18, 1931, Thomas Alva Edison, died at age eighty-four. Reporters scrambled to get the news of his death out to their readers. "The light-bearer has gone into the darkness," blared one newspaper headline. "An Inspirer, One of our Immortals, the Conqueror of the Unknown has left our midst," declared another.

In reporting on his death, many newspapers and news reports would quote from Thomas Edison's last public speech to the National Electric Light Association. "My message to you is to be courageous. I have lived a long time. I have seen history repeat itself again and again. I have seen many depressions in business. Always America has come out stronger and more prosperous. Be as brave as your fathers before you. Have faith. Go forward."

Adair, Gene. *Thomas Alva Edison: Inventing the Electric Age.* New York: Oxford University Press, 1996.

Baldwin, Neil. *Edison: Inventing the Century.* New York: Hyperion, 1995.

Buranelli, Vincent. *Thomas Alva Edison.* Englewood Cliffs, NJ: Silver Burdett, 1989.

Conot, Robert. *A Streak of Luck.* New York: Seaview Books, 1979.

Cramer, Carol, ed. *Thomas Edison.* San Diego, CA: Greenhaven Press, 2001.

Egan, Louise. *Thomas Edison: The Great American Inventor.* Hauppauge, NY: Barron's Educational Series, 1987.

Janet and Geoff Benge are a husband and wife writing team with more than thirty years of writing experience. Janet is a former elementary school teacher. Geoff holds a degree in history. Together they have a passion to make history come alive for a new generation of readers.

Originally from New Zealand, the Benges make their home in the Orlando, Florida, area.

HEROES OF HISTORY are available in paperback, e-book, and audiobook formats, with more coming soon! Unit Study Curriculum Guides are available for each biography.

www.HeroesThenAndNow.com

Also from Janet and Geoff Benge...
More adventure-filled biographies for ages 10 to 100!

Heroes of History

George Washington Carver: From Slave to Scientist • *978-1-883002-78-7*
Abraham Lincoln: A New Birth of Freedom • *978-1-883002-79-4*
Meriwether Lewis: Off the Edge of the Map • *978-1-883002-80-0*
George Washington: True Patriot • *978-1-883002-81-7*
William Penn: Liberty and Justice for All • *978-1-883002-82-4*
Harriet Tubman: Freedombound • *978-1-883002-90-9*
John Adams: Independence Forever • *978-1-883002-51-0*
Clara Barton: Courage under Fire • *978-1-883002-50-3*
Daniel Boone: Frontiersman • *978-1-932096-09-5*
Theodore Roosevelt: An American Original • *978-1-932096-10-1*
Douglas MacArthur: What Greater Honor • *978-1-932096-15-6*
Benjamin Franklin: Live Wire • *978-1-932096-14-9*
Christopher Columbus: Across the Ocean Sea • *978-1-932096-23-1*
Laura Ingalls Wilder: A Storybook Life • *978-1-932096-32-3*
Orville Wright: The Flyer • *978-1-932096-34-7*
John Smith: A Foothold in the New World • *978-1-932096-36-1*
Thomas Edison: Inspiration and Hard Work • *978-1-932096-37-8*
Alan Shepard: Higher and Faster • *978-1-932096-41-5*
Ronald Reagan: Destiny at His Side • *978-1-932096-65-1*
Davy Crockett: Ever Westward • *978-1-932096-67-5*
Milton Hershey: More Than Chocolate • *978-1-932096-82-8*
Billy Graham: America's Pastor • *978-1-62486-024-9*
Ben Carson: A Chance at Life • *978-1-62486-034-8*
Louis Zamperini: Redemption • *978-1-62486-049-2*
Elizabeth Fry: Angel of Newgate • *978-1-62486-064-5*
William Wilberforce: Take Up the Fight • *978-1-62486-057-7*

Christian Heroes: Then & Now

Gladys Aylward: The Adventure of a Lifetime • *978-1-57658-019-6*
Nate Saint: On a Wing and a Prayer • *978-1-57658-017-2*
Hudson Taylor: Deep in the Heart of China • *978-1-57658-016-5*
Amy Carmichael: Rescuer of Precious Gems • *978-1-57658-018-9*
Eric Liddell: Something Greater Than Gold • *978-1-57658-137-7*
Corrie ten Boom: Keeper of the Angels' Den • *978-1-57658-136-0*
William Carey: Obliged to Go • *978-1-57658-147-6*
George Müller: Guardian of Bristol's Orphans • *978-1-57658-145-2*

Jim Elliot: One Great Purpose • 978-1-57658-146-9
Mary Slessor: Forward into Calabar • 978-1-57658-148-3
David Livingstone: Africa's Trailblazer • 978-1-57658-153-7
Betty Greene: Wings to Serve • 978-1-57658-152-0
Adoniram Judson: Bound for Burma • 978-1-57658-161-2
Cameron Townsend: Good News in Every Language • 978-1-57658-164-3
Jonathan Goforth: An Open Door in China • 978-1-57658-174-2
Lottie Moon: Giving Her All for China • 978-1-57658-188-9
John Williams: Messenger of Peace • 978-1-57658-256-5
William Booth: Soup, Soap, and Salvation • 978-1-57658-258-9
Rowland Bingham: Into Africa's Interior • 978-1-57658-282-4
Ida Scudder: Healing Bodies, Touching Hearts • 978-1-57658-285-5
Wilfred Grenfell: Fisher of Men • 978-1-57658-292-3
Lillian Trasher: The Greatest Wonder in Egypt • 978-1-57658-305-0
Loren Cunningham: Into All the World • 978-1-57658-199-5
Florence Young: Mission Accomplished • 978-1-57658-313-5
Sundar Singh: Footprints Over the Mountains • 978-1-57658-318-0
C. T. Studd: No Retreat • 978-1-57658-288-6
Rachel Saint: A Star in the Jungle • 978-1-57658-337-1
Brother Andrew: God's Secret Agent • 978-1-57658-355-5
Clarence Jones: Mr. Radio • 978-1-57658-343-2
Count Zinzendorf: Firstfruit • 978-1-57658-262-6
John Wesley: The World His Parish • 978-1-57658-382-1
C. S. Lewis: Master Storyteller • 978-1-57658-385-2
David Bussau: Facing the World Head-on • 978-1-57658-415-6
Jacob DeShazer: Forgive Your Enemies • 978-1-57658-475-0
Isobel Kuhn: On the Roof of the World • 978-1-57658-497-2
Elisabeth Elliot: Joyful Surrender • 978-1-57658-513-9
Paul Brand: Helping Hands • 978-1-57658-536-8
D. L. Moody: Bringing Souls to Christ • 978-1-57658-552-8
Dietrich Bonhoeffer: In the Midst of Wickedness • 978-1-57658-713-3
Francis Asbury: Circuit Rider • 978-1-57658-737-9
Samuel Zwemer: The Burden of Arabia • 978-1-57658-738-6
Klaus-Dieter John: Hope in the Land of the Incas • 978-1-57658-826-2
Mildred Cable: Through the Jade Gate • 978-157658-886-4

Available in paperback, e-book, and audiobook formats.
Unit Study Curriculum Guides are available for many biographies.
www.HeroesThenAndNow.com